All-Terrain Pushchair Walks

North Hampshire

Jane F Ward

© Jane F Ward, 2012

Jane F Ward has asserted her moral rights to be identified as the author of this work in accordance with the Copyright, Designs and Patents Act 1988.

Published by Sigma Leisure – an imprint of
Sigma Press, Stobart House, Pontyclerc, Penybanc Road
Ammanford, Carmarthenshire SA18 3HP

British Library Cataloguing in Publication Data

A CIP record for this book is available from the British Library

ISBN: 978-1-85058-907-5

Typesetting and Design by: Sigma Press, Ammanford, Carms

Maps: Bute Cartographics

Photographs: Jane F Ward

Cover phototgraph: The view from Ladle Hill looking across to Beacon Hill

Printed by: Berforts Group Limited

Disclaimer: The information in this book is given in good faith and is believed to be correct at the time of publication. Care should always be taken when walking in hill country. Where appropriate, attention has been drawn to matters of safety. The author and publisher cannot take responsibility for any accidents or injury incurred whilst following these walks. Only you can judge your own fitness, competence and experience. Do not rely solely on sketch maps for navigation: we strongly recommend the use of appropriate Ordnance Survey (or equivalent) maps.

Preface

North Hampshire provides an ideal area to introduce your children to the great outdoors. You don't have to travel far to reach some beautiful and varied countryside, with a wealth of wildlife, packed full of historical or literary reference. Furthermore, you are never far from a diversity of attractions or a bustling market town to complete your day out.

This book was initiated to provide walks for mothers wanting to regain a level of fitness after pregnancy without resorting to expensive gym membership, personal trainers and without the added headache of finding suitable childcare. Whether you're walking as a family, a group, with other parents or just with your little one, getting out into the fresh air can invigorate mind and body and bring the sense of well being needed to cope with interrupted sleep and early mornings enjoyed during early parenting.

The walks selected for this book are intended to be suitable for all-terrain three wheel pushchairs. You may be able to get away with a robust stroller on a few of the easier walks but the majority would be very hard going without the larger wheels of an all-terrain pushchair. If you're walking with a very young baby you should select easier walks as young babies are not suited to being bumped about too much.

We would suggest that anyone using this guide book should try an easier walk to start with, not just so you can build your fitness to cope with the more difficult walks, but also so you can gauge the grading used and to gain experience in pushing and controlling your pushchair over varied terrain.

Finally we hope that you enjoy the walks as much as we've enjoyed discovering them.

Jane and Annabelle

Acknowledgements

I am grateful to everyone who has suggested walks and walked with me during the production of this book. In particular I'd like to thank Annabelle, my daughter, for accompanying me on all of the walks. I would also like to thank Penny Billingham, her daughter Rose, Dawn West, her son Owen, and her West Highland Terrier Presley, Debbie Smith and her daughter Katie, all of whom have been of great help in suggesting routes and for accompanying us on many of the walks. I would also like to thank everyone who helped to trial the walks; their comments have been extremely useful.

Supporting Charity

During September and October 2010 I undertook a sponsored walk of all 30 walks included in this guide book, covering over 100 miles, with my daughter Annabelle, to raise money for Breast Cancer Campaign. I would like to thank everyone who supported us in raising funds for this worthy charity. Particular thanks go to The George Inn in Vernham Dean (Walk 1), Marwell Wildlife Park near Winchester (Walk 15), Bird World near Farnham (Walk 22), and Wellington Country Park near Reading (Walk 29) for their generosity. More details for these venues can be found within the walk descriptions.

Contents

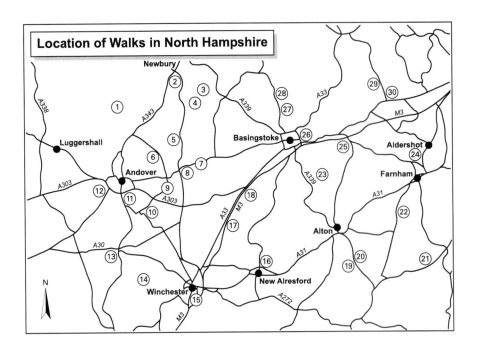

Location of Walks in North Hampshire

Walk Index

Total Climb is the approximate cumulative climb during the walk.
Grade is the relative difficulty of the walk as compared to the other walks in this book. Walks graded ★ are likely to be shorter, easier and with little ascent, whereas walks graded ★★★★★ are likely to be longer and more difficult, either due to the terrain or the total ascent during the walk. There is one walk graded ★★★★★★ that includes a number of climbs and is relatively long.

The Countryside Code

The Countryside Code applies to all parts of the countryside in England and Wales. Most of the code is just good commonsense helping us respect, protect and enjoy the countryside.
Five sections are dedicated to members of the general public:

Be safe, plan ahead and follow any signs
- be prepared for changes in weather and other events
- check weather conditions before you go, and don't be afraid to turn back
- let someone know where you're going and when you expect to return

Leave gates and property as you find them
- leave gates as you find them or follow instructions on signs
- in fields with crops follow the paths closely
- use gates, stiles or gaps in field boundaries when provided

Protect plants and animals and take your litter home
- give wild and farm animals plenty of space, especially if they have young
- be careful not to drop a match or smouldering cigarette

Keep dogs under close control
- keep your dog on a short lead on areas of open country and common land between 1 March and 31 July, and all year round near farm animals
- keep your dog on a lead if you cannot rely on its obedience
- if a farm animal chases you and your dog, it is safer to let your dog off the lead, don't risk getting hurt by trying to protect it
- take dog mess home or use a purpose built bin if available

Consider other people
- respect the needs of local people, don't block gateways, driveways or other entry points with your vehicle
- support the rural economy by getting your supplies from local outlets
- Keep out of the way when farm animals are being gathered or moved
- when riding a bike or driving a vehicle, slow down for horses, walkers and livestock and give them plenty of room

Whether you're walking along remote hill tops or taking an amble along one of Hampshire's beautiful rivers, use your common sense to apply the principles of the country code. Teach your children to enjoy the countryside and to treat it with respect by following the countryside code.

Introduction to North Hampshire

It's easy to live in North Hampshire in the belief that it's a landscape of rolling motorways and bustling market towns without fully appreciating the variety of beautiful, tranquil and unspoilt retreats. It's not until you start to explore the area that you'll find the wealth of heathland, ancient forest, spectacular uplands of outstanding natural beauty and miles of footpaths, bridleways and byways. In addition there's a treasury of quintessential English villages, complete with picturesque timber frame and thatched cottages, country pubs serving good home cooked food, meandering rivers with vintage mills, glorious gardens, pretty village duck ponds and historic country churches.

Furthermore, the area offers visitors and locals alike a wide range of things to do and award-winning attractions. You can visit the ancestral homes of Dukes or see where historic figures like Jane Austen, Charles Kingsley and Gilbert White spent their lives. There are also many events throughout the year and plenty of all-weather family activities.

North Hampshire offers visitors miles of idyllic countryside to explore, stretching from the South Downs National Park in the east to the North Wessex Downs in the north of the county. With its unique mixture of rolling hills, chalk streams, country parks and bustling market towns, North Hampshire's countryside is the perfect destination for a family visit.

Stately Homes and Gardens

North Hampshire has been home to some of Britain's greatest historical and literary figures, and many of the houses and gardens in which they lived are open for you to enjoy.

Choose from grand stately homes such as Northington Grange near Alresford, where they hold spectacular opera events, and Stratfield Saye House, which became the Duke of Wellington's country estate in 1817 after his victory at Waterloo, or the more intimate houses such as Jane Austen's home at Chawton, near Alton, and naturalist Gilbert White's House and gardens, which can be visited in the charming village of Selborne.

There is also a wealth of gardening history in North Hampshire including Queen Eleanor's Garden at the Great Hall in Winchester, which is a charming re-creation of a medieval herbarium sanctuary, while The Vyne near Basingstoke offers five centuries of history in over a thousand acres of gardens and parkland.

Literary Connections

It was the Watership Downs in North Hampshire on which the famous book by Richard Adams, *Watership Down* was based. Indeed Nuthanger Farm, just south of Ecchinswell is featured in his famous book. Richard Adams grew up in the area so was able to use the breathtaking views as stimulation for his novel.

In the east of the county you can follow in the footsteps of Flora Thompson and poet Alfred Lord Tennyson, as they walked alongside the tranquil Waggoner's Wells in Greyshott. And in Winchester you can be inspired like the romantic poet John Keats, in his daily walk though the Cathedral Close and water meadows to St Cross Hospital, which led to his ode To Autumn.

Market Towns

In the towns of North Hampshire you'll find fascinating historic buildings and museums, many of which have regular markets. The Hampshire Farmers' Markets tours the county, offering tempting local produce such as sausages, smoked trout, chutneys, honey and organic meats.

Farmers' market at Winchester

Why Walk?

Once you've welcomed your new baby into the world and want to regain or improve your fitness levels, forget expensive gym membership or sweaty aerobics classes and the strain of finding a crèche or babysitter, just get out in the fresh air and push your little one up some hills. Start slowly with short distances on easier ground, then as your fitness and your baby's resilience improves, and you can go for longer between feeds, building up to more adventurous countryside rambles.

Walking with your children is a great way of exploring both your local area and new places, it gives you time to take in your surroundings and to teach your little ones to enjoy the countryside. There's also great value in teaming up with other recent parents, not only can you keep each other motivated but you can relax, chat and compare notes on caring for a new baby.

Walking is one of the easiest ways to be physically active and is a great way of getting your recommended daily exercise. It needs no specialist equipment – just a good pair of sturdy shoes or boots and a suitable pushchair. Walking burns as many calories as jogging over the same distance and, because it's a low impact exercise, it won't stress your joints; in fact it's great for strengthening muscles, bones and joints.

Research has shown that regular walking can:

- Lift your mood and can make you feel positive
- Reduce stress by releasing the 'feel good hormones', endorphins, thus overcoming the stresses and strains of everyday life, improve your sense of well-being and help you sleep better
- Help you to manage your weight
- Increase your stamina and energy levels
- Increase your fitness and improve lung capacity
- Burn the same calories as jogging
- Halve the risk of heart disease, reduce blood pressure, and reduce the risk of a stroke
- Improve the immune system and can reduce the risk of some cancers
- Lower your cholesterol and help prevent diabetes

The All-Terrain Pushchair

Before venturing off road with your little one, make sure that you have a pushchair that is designed for the terrain you'll be covering. There are many pushchair designs on the market, but if you're looking for a proper all-terrain pushchair it will have three large wheels, pneumatic tyres and good suspension.

It is the size of wheels and the single front wheel which allows the all-terrain pushchair to negotiate uneven ground more easily than its urban counterpart. Other factors such as a long wheel base and a fixed (or lockable) front wheel will allow for better obstacle negotiation, and a light weight frame will add to the overall performance of the pushchair.

The suspension and pneumatic tyres provide a degree of cushioning for your baby (to avoid frequent punctures its worth fitting your tyres with Kevlar or similar tyre liners). However, very young babies shouldn't be bounced about too much, so stick to the easier walks until they're at least four months old.

Another important consideration, especially if you are going off road with a young baby, is to have a fully reclining seat and a padded or sheepskin lining to provide comfortable and cosy accommodation.

It should go without saying that any all-terrain pushchair should have a five point safety harness. Other essential accessories include a warm and windproof footmuff, rain cover, sun shield, puncture repair kit, pump and a pushchair leash. A pushchair leash is essential for off road use to ensure that the pushchair stays with you if you accidently slip or let go of the pushchair on sloping ground. It is also much safer than a brake which can be accidently disengaged during a rest stop.

Photo of my all-terrain pushchair at Caesars Camp with far reaching views over Aldershot

Walking Safety

Walking is an easily accessible pastime; you can safely walk in towns or easy countryside without specialist clothing or equipment. If you intend to go further into the countryside, you should take a little time to prepare and follow a few simple rules:

- Don't tackle overly long or difficult routes for your own level of fitness or experience or for your baby's age and resilience to being bumped about in a pushchair. Turn back if the terrain is unsuitable

- Unless you're very familiar with the area, take a map, guidebooks, compass or navigation equipment

- Make sure you and your charge are adequately dressed for the length of time you'll be out. Take extra clothing and a footmuff, especially in winter months. In summer months always carry sun cream, sun hats and a sun shield for the pushchair

- Check the forecast before you set out, and always take a waterproof for yourself and a rain cover for your pushchair. Keep an eye on the weather and don't be afraid to head back if things change

- Take sufficient water and/or milk for for your child and yourself

- Take adequate food for your little ones and yourself, unless you're absolutely sure you'll be able to obtain food on route or you don't plan to be out for very long. At any rate you should carry emergency rations

- Take a changing bag, first aid kit, any medicines you might need and a puncture repair kit and pump

- On longer or more difficult walks, have a contingency short route back, in case you need to end your walk for whatever reason

- Make sure someone knows when you expect to be back

- Take a mobile phone but be aware that coverage may not be great in some areas

- Always use a pushchair leash, attaching the pushchair to your wrist on all but the easiest walks

The golden rule is, make sure that both your little one and you are comfortable, dressed for the sort of weather and terrain you are likely to meet, and that you never underestimate the changeability of British weather!

Walking off road

When walking over an uneven surface, or ground with roots or stones, take care to ensure your pushchair doesn't tip over. Three-wheel pushchairs are generally stable on reasonably smooth terrain but if a rear wheel is raised more than a few inches relative to the other, there is a risk that the pushchair could tip over. It's suggested that you keep a firm grip on your pushchair using both hands.

If you're walking up or down slopes or hills, it is recommended that you attach your pushchair to your wrist using a pushchair leash. Many all-terrain pushchairs come equipped with a suitable leash but if not they can be purchased separately.

Walking on roads

If you're walking on roads even for a short section, follow the advice set out in the Highway Code: use the pavement if there is one; try to make yourself visible to drivers; where there is no pavement walk on the right facing oncoming traffic, and cross to the other side well before sharp right-hand bends; take special care on country roads with no pavements where traffic may be moving very fast.

Livestock

You should use your own judgement and common sense about entering a field which contains livestock with a pushchair, especially if you also have a dog. If there's a herd of cattle near the footpath, it might be sensible to deviate away from them to cross the field. Generally if you move quietly without rushing, you will not attract their attention, but if you are concerned about a particular situation keep calm and try not to do anything to excite them. Use an ordinary speaking voice rather than shouting and don't brandish a stick or umbrella. Livestock can often be deterred from following you too closely by turning to face them with both arms raised. Don't walk between a cow and her calf or a bull and his wives. If you are threatened by cattle when walking a dog, you should let the dog off the lead so that it draws them away from you.

In late spring and early summer you should be aware of ticks especially if you walk through rough vegetation, particularly in places where deer live. If you find a tick attached to your (or your baby's) skin, remove it immediately, preferably with tweezers, pulling firmly and steadily so that it disengages itself. After your walk, carefully examine your own and your baby's body for ticks and, if you think you or your baby have been bitten, seek medical advice indicating that you are concerned about the risk of Lyme disease.

More information about health and safety for walkers can be found at www.ramblers.org.uk

How to use this book

It's hoped that readers will find this book to have an intuitive lay out and to be easy to use. There's a map index showing the location of all the walks at the front of the book and an index of the walks giving specific details to help you select a suitable walk. The main part of the book is dedicated to individual walk descriptions, each of which has a sketch map to assist you as you follow the narrative.

At the start of each walk description some key features are given so that you can quickly judge whether the walk is suitable for your requirements. In the paragraphs below these features and other information set out in the walk descriptions are briefly described so that the information can be used effectively.

Distance
The distance given is an indication of the length of the walk in miles. The measurement allows comparison between walks but is not meant to provide a highly accurate measure of the distance walked.

Time taken
The time taken is a rough estimate of how long the walk might take if a consistent and reasonably enthusiastic pace is maintained. The walks may take significantly longer if completed at a leisurely pace or if toddlers are allowed to walk. The time given doesn't include long rest stops but does include breather stops to appreciate the view after any hilly sections. You should allow plenty of time to complete the walks bearing in mind your own fitness level and your natural walking pace.

Grade
Each walk is given a grade for overall difficulty, scoring one star for an easy walk through to six stars for the more difficult ones. The grade is an objective feel for the overall difficulty of the walk, depending on distance and ascent but also by a number of other variables, such as the surface underfoot. It's much harder work to push a pushchair along a sand path than a tarmac one, and roots and stones can make the going quite awkward. A brief description of the terrain is also given.

Total climb
Total climb indicates the cumulative height climbed during the walk. For any given height climbed, it could comprise of a number of smaller undulations spread across the walk or a concentration of more significant efforts interrupting an otherwise flat walk.

The data given is subject to error due to the fairly course sampling interval used in obtaining data. It is possible that for example, where a crest of a hill is reached and a descent started within a sampling interval the full height of the crest will not be counted. Hence, where a route is highly undulating the data could under estimate the actual total height climbed during a walk.

Postcode
The postcode listed is the nearest postcode to the start of the walk. It cannot always be used in isolation from other means of navigation to locate the start point due to the larger areas covered by each postcode in rural areas. Satellite navigation should be used in conjunction with a map of the destination.

Grid Reference
All of the walks in this guide book start from a grid reference beginning with the letters SU as they are within the 100km by 100km square of Britain thus labelled. The six digits refer to distances from the south west corner (or origin) of this square, to determine a 100 m square. The first three digits refer to the distance east, and the second three digits refer to the distance north, from the south west corner.

More information about coordinate systems in Great Britain can be found on the Ordinance Survey website in a document entitled *A Guide to Coordinate Systems in Great Britain.*

Ordinance Survey Explorer Map
There should be sufficient detail in the walk descriptions for you to find your way, however, it is recommended that you always carry a detailed map of the area as back up. OS Explorer Maps 1:25000 scale, are specially designed for walkers and others involved in outdoor activities. The level of detail is ideal for walking with places of interest, picnic areas, viewpoints, rights of way, National Trail and Recreational Path routes all marked.

Terrain
The terrain of the walk is briefly described, listing the nature of the paths or tracks together with any difficult sections, such as uneven paths prone to becoming muddy. This section is not exhaustive as the walks have not been tried in all possible conditions. It should also be noted that the nature of any route may change over time or may be subject to unexpected factors, such as a blocked drain or a fallen tree.

Obstacles
Any obstacles which need to be negotiated are listed together with notes on how the obstacle was tackled during the trial walks. For safety reasons two people are recommended for any of the walks which have one or more obstacles. The safety of your child is, of course, your own responsibility, and

you may consider that it's safer for your little one to disembark whilst the pushchair is lifted through or over a particular obstacle.

Parking
This section provides a brief description of how to get to the starting point, including a suggestion of where to park if you have travelled by car. This in no way guarantees the safety of the parking area; drivers are responsible for the safety of their own vehicle.

Walk Description
Walk descriptions and route diagrams are fairly detailed and should provide sufficient information for users to find their way. However, it is recommended that the information is used in conjunction with an appropriate Ordinance Survey map. Most of the routes are circular and are written to be followed in the direction indicated. It is not recommended that routes be attempted in the opposite direction as they may be significantly more difficult in reverse.

Each walk starts from the described parking area and is marked on the associated diagram with the letter 'S'. Thereafter each section of the route corresponds to a numerical point on the diagram.

The narrative is heavily punctuated with the number of yards taken. This measure is given to provide an indication of distance between described landmarks, indeed where landmarks are in short supply the number of yards should assist in identifying the location of points of action, such as turning left or right. The number of yards is not intended to be highly accurate but rather to be used as an approximate or comparative measure. If yards are not your preferred unit of measure, they're fairly comparable to metres, 1 yard = 0.91 metres.

Refreshments
At the end of each walk description an establishment serving refreshments is given. It's advisable to check their opening times before setting out as not all are open all day. In many cases the listed local attractions also have an associated café.

Local attractions
Each walk has at least one attraction listed. However, it's worth checking the attractions listed under a few walks in the region so that you can choose ones that are most suitable. Attractions such as Finkley Farm, near Andover, are very popular with youngsters and may tick more boxes than the attraction listed with your selected walk. All of the attractions are worth a visit if you're in the area, some can take a good part of the day, whilst others may only require a short visit. If you mix and match walks and attractions you can create your own tailor-made day out.

Accuracy

While every care has been taken to ensure the accuracy of the information included in this book, neither the publisher nor the author can accept responsibility for errors or omissions, or for changes in the details provided or for the consequences of any reliance on the information provided. The countryside is dynamic: field boundaries, fences and hedges can be altered; footpaths can be rerouted and concessionary paths may be closed or diverted. In addition footpaths and tracks that are pleasant for walking in good conditions may become muddy, slippery and hard going in wet weather.

If you do find an inaccuracy in either the text or maps, please write to Sigma Press providing details of the inaccuracies encountered.

1. Vernham Dean

Distance	3.6 miles (5.8km)	Time taken	1 hour 15 mins
Grade	★ ★ ★	Postcode	SP11 0HB
Grid Ref	SU345563	Total climb	205 ft (62m)
Map	Ordnance Survey Explorer Map: 1:25000 scale – Sheet 131		
Terrain	Country roads, tracks and footpaths. The byway along the northern section of this walk is stony in places		
Obstacles	None		
Parking	Vernham Dean is situated 8 miles north of Andover. Turn off the A343 in Hurstbourne Tarrant onto Back Lane. Continue for 3.4 miles, passing through Ibthorpe and Upton. As you approach Vernham Dean turn right into the village playing fields, just before the primary school		

The picturesque village of Vernham Dean is a conservation area lying in the North Wessex Downs Area of Outstanding Natural Beauty. The village has a long history, indeed the name Vernham is derived from the Anglo-Saxon Fernham meaning 'enclosed against the bracken', and Dean from Dene meaning 'a valley'. Aerial photographs of the area have revealed sites of Iron and Roman Age settlements, the best preserved of which is at Boat Copse to the south west of the village.

The route starts at the village playing fields, next to the primary school and goes through the village past the George Inn. This 17th century inn is now tiled but its roof has the characteristic curved shape of previous being thatched. The route then follows a pretty byway, passing arable fields which blossom with red poppies during summer months, and continues along a farm track, known as Church Lane, and past Box Farm which has organic free range eggs available from a wooden box in front of the house. The route then proceeds along undulating lanes and farm tracks as it gradually climbs to higher ground. Listen out for the cries of red kite and, with luck, you'll see them hunting or displaying above these quiet tracks.

The route emerges near St. Mary's Church, which although added to over the years, has Norman or perhaps Saxon foundations. Indeed the thick west wall and the zig-zag mouldings around the entrance door are typical Norman work. At a vantage point just after the church there are wonderful views over

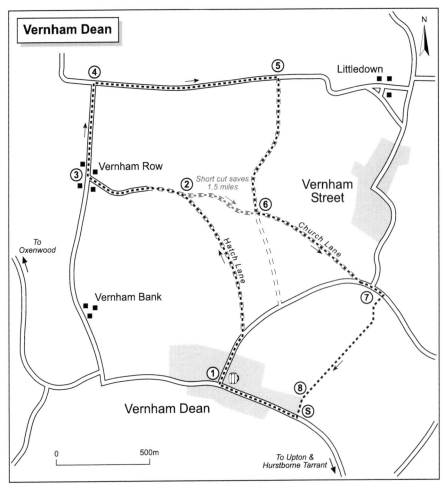

the Swift Valley towards Hurstbourne Tarrant, Chute Causeway and Haydown Hill. From here the route follows a footpath back down to the starting point, at the village playing field, where there's a children's play ground.

Walk description

S. Leave the Village Playing Field, with the primary school on your right, and turn right onto the road to walk along the pavement towards Vernham Dean. After 250 yards, continue straight on past the top of Shepherds Rise. After another 40 yards the pavement runs out, so take care along this short section past the village hall.

1. After 150 yards, immediately after the George Inn, turn right and walk up Bulpitts Hill. After 275 yards, turn left into Hatchbury Lane, which after 50 yards becomes a grass track between hedges, signed 'Restricted Byway'. Follow this track up a gentle gradient. The arable field on your right is a sea of poppies in the summer which you can glimpse though gateways.

2. After 815 yards, turn left at a junction onto a gravel farm track, Church Lane. Follow this track up a gentle gradient, after 220 yards passing Box Farm. Continue for a further 325 yards, along a tarmac drive down hill to Bowers Lane.

St Mary's Church door with Norman zig-zag moulding

3. Turn right onto Bowers Lane, passing the entrance to Gambles Cottage on your left, and continue straight on along this pretty country road under overhanging trees.

4. After 550 yards, where the road bends sharply left, turn right onto a grass track (signed 'Restricted Byway') to go under electricity cables. This track is a little uneven to start. After 300 yards, continue straight on past a grass track on your right, and after another 315 yards, keep right where the track forks. After a further 250 yards, continue up a short stony hill.

5. Then after 215 yards, at a crossing of tracks, turn right and follow another track down a gentle hill. You may catch a glimpse of red kite over the fields to your right.

6. After 665 yards you'll walk under electricity cables, then after another 185 yards, at a crossing of tracks, turn left into Church Lane (signed 'Restricted Byway'). During summer months this footpath is beautiful with a myriad of hedgerow flowers. After 775 yards, after passing a number of horse paddocks, bear left to join a country road. Take care as visibility is limited.

7. After 70 yards, at a junction where the road bends to the left, continue straight on, signed 'Church' (and 'Upton' on a sign post in the hedge to

your right). After another 85 yards, just before the Church, turn right onto a signed footpath. Continue past the church yard on your left, then after 135 yards, as you come into a field, bear slightly right to find a mown path between two arable fields.

Continue along this path, with the fence which marks the field boundary on your right, and on down the hill. This section offers great views over the surrounding countryside. After 285 yards, continue through a tunnel of black/hawthorn bushes.

8. Then after another 300 yards, at the bottom of the hill, go through a gap in the fence line into the children's play ground and back to the playing field car park at the starting point.

Refreshments

The George Inn
Vernham Dean, Andover SP11 0JY
This is an old-fashioned village pub dating back to the 17th century, with fireplaces, oak beams and an attractive beer garden. The pub has an excellent reputation for a warm welcome, freshly-cooked, quality food and real ale. Children and dogs are welcome.
www.thegeorgeatvernhamdean.co.uk

The 17th century George Inn at Vernham Dean

Attractions

Wilton Windmill (6.5 miles)
Wilton Down Road, Wilton SN8 3SP
Wilton Windmill stands on a site that provides magnificent views of the surrounding hills. The mill is the only working windmill in Wessex and was originally constructed in 1821. It's open for guided tours on Sundays and Bank Holiday Mondays between 2pm and 5pm, from Easter until the end of September.
www.wiltonwindmill.co.uk

Crofton Beam Engines (8.5 miles)
Crofton Pumping Station, Crofton, Marlborough SN8 3DN
Crofton Pumping Station was built in 1807 to provide water to the summit of the Kennet and Avon Canal. This Grade I listed building houses two magnificent Cornish beam engines, one of which is the oldest working beam engine in the

Wilton Windmill originally constructed in 1821

world. Fresh, locally prepared food is available in the café, and there is plenty of room in the grounds for sitting and enjoying the splendid views. Open April – September.
www.croftonbeamengines.org

Ludgershall Castle and Cross (8.5 miles)
Castle Street, Ludgershall SP11 9QT
These ruins and earthworks are of a royal castle, frequently used as a hunting lodge, dating mainly from the 12th and 13th centuries. It's thought that the castle's southern enclosure was formed out of the surviving earthworks of an Iron Age hill fort. The remains of the medieval cross stand in the centre of the village.
www.historicbritain.com/vendor/ludgershall.aspx

2. Great Penwood

Distance	2 miles (3km)	Time taken	1 hour
Grade	★	Postcode	RG20 0LT
Grid Ref	SU452621	Total climb	100 ft (30m)
Map	Ordnance Survey Explorer Map: 1:25000 scale - Sheet 158		
Terrain	Gravel tracks and paths. In wet weather some of the unsurfaced paths can get very muddy		
Obstacles	At the end of the full walk there's a fairly low metal barrier to push under to get back into the parking area. Take care that you have plenty of clearance; if in doubt take your little one out of the pushchair before pushing under the barrier		
Parking	Great Penwood is situated 3 miles south west of Newbury, and just north of Highclere Castle. From Tothill Services take the B4640 towards Whitway/Burghclere. After 0.4 miles, turn right at the junction. Then after 0.1 miles, turn right again to cross the A34. Then, after 1 mile, turn right signed to Penwood Nursery. After 0.5 miles turn left into an off road car parking area		

Great Penwood is a mixed conifer and deciduous woodland, formerly owned by the Carnarvon Estates but purchased by the Forestry Commission in 1955. Now commercially managed, Penwood is a Site of Importance for Nature Conservation, within the North Wessex Downs Area of Outstanding Natural Beauty. These woods are popular with dog walkers come rain or sunshine. The area is rich in wildlife and has a wide range of interesting trees, including holly, beech and white poplars. In parts of the wood there's a fairly significant infestation of rhododendron, first introduced to Britain in the late 18th Century. Although beautiful when in flower, its dense foliage out competes native species and its leaves are unpalatable to most herbivores, leading to a diminishing biodiversity.

Penwood has a long section of gravel surfaced track leading away from the parking area which facilitates walking in all weather conditions. There's also a network of unsurfaced tracks and paths throughout the woods, some of which are suitable for pushchairs for much of the year. The route starts along a sweeping gravel track which leads into the heart of the wood, then follows footpaths and grass tracks between large rhododendron bushes, and continues along another gravel track through an area of regeneration that attracts a wealth of bird life, including woodpeckers and kestrels. If it's wet underfoot, the route is best finished back along the same gravel track on which it started, as the footpaths can get very muddy.

Walk Description

S. From the road walk through the parking area, bearing left to find a metal barrier with a 'No Motorcycles' sign on its left. Follow a footpath around the right hand side of the barrier to access a wide gravel track. Follow this track as it bears left then, after 150 yards as it sweeps round to the right.

1. After another 135 yards, continue straight on past a gravel track on the right, then after 175 yards follow the track over a large ditch and on past a track to your left. After a further 75 yards continue straight on past a track to your right and follow the track up a gentle incline through the trees.

2. After 300 yards, at a crossing of tracks, just before the track climbs a little steeper, turn left onto a narrowing path (there's a huge conifer on your right 35 yards after making this turning). Continue along this footpath on a slight incline towards houses ahead. The trees on your right are covered with the bright orange *Trentepholia* algae which is not harmful to the trees.

3. After 365 yards, as you approach the first of the houses, follow the path as it bears right up another slight incline, and then continue straight on as the path runs adjacent to a row of garden fences.

4. After 335 yards, turn right just before the last house, adjacent to a wooden gate to your left. Follow this path and after 135 yards, continue past a large aerial mast on your left, then after another 265 yards continue straight on past a turning to your left.

5. After a further 85 yards, at a junction with a wide gravel track, continue straight on to walk across the top of the gravel track, to follow a footpath with grass verges on both sides (or take the short cut described below). Continue straight on along this path, then after 345 yards follow the path as it turns right and continues down a slight decline.

6. After 85 yards, at a junction, turn right onto a grass track. Then after 145 yards pass a large holly bush (set back from the track) to your left, and after another 25 yards, turn left onto a footpath between large rhododendron bushes. In winter months this path is muddy. Continue for 35 yards then follow the path as it turns to the right. In early summer the rhododendron bushes are beautiful in bloom, attracting many

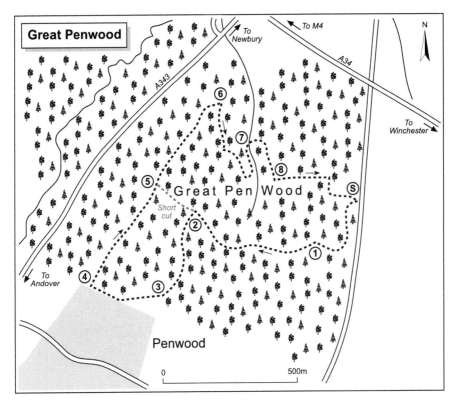

bumble bees. Continue for another 115 yards to follow the path as it turns to the left.

7. After 130 yards, the path crosses a tiny stream that feeds a small pond on your left (in all but the driest conditions). In summer damselflies may be seen here. After 15 yards, bear right at a fork to walk between more rhododendron bushes, then after another 40 yards, bear right at a second fork.

8. After 145 yards, the path emerges onto a gravel track. Turn left to follow the track up a short slope, then after 220 yards, turn right at a fork onto another gravel track. After another 20 yards, turn left to follow the track back towards the parking area. After 105 yards, push your pushchair under a fairly low metal barrier (obstacle) into the parking area at the start point.

Short cut at point 5
At point 5 if you wish to take a short cut and avoid paths which can be muddy in wet weather, turn right to follow the track down the hill. After

200 yards you'll reach the crossing of tracks at point 2. Continue straight on to retrace your steps along the gravel track back to the car parking area after 865 yards.

Refreshments

The Carnarvon Arms

Winchester Rd, Whitway, Burghclere, Newbury RG20 9LE
The Carnarvon Arms is grade II listed, built in the 1800s as a coaching Inn providing a stop off for travellers to nearby Highclere Castle. It is now beautifully renovated offering a stunning dining room with a high vaulted ceiling and a thriving friendly bar. Their menus feature imaginative modern British à la carte dishes, as well as traditional pub classics.
www.carnarvonarms.com

Local Attractions

Highclere Castle (2 miles)

Highclere Park, Newbury RG20 9RN
Highclere is one of England's most beautiful Victorian Castles set amidst 1,000 acres of spectacular Parkland. The Carnarvon family has lived at Highclere since 1679, although records show the castle itself stands on the site of an earlier house, which in turn was built on the foundations of the medieval palace owned by the Bishops of Winchester. Open from Easter to Autumn.
www.highclerecastle.co.uk

The area of regeneration is abundant with wildlife

3. Ecchinswell and Nuthanger Farm

Distance	3.8 miles (6.1km)	Time taken	2 hours
Grade	★ ★ ★ ★ ★	Postcode	RG20 4UH
Grid Ref	SU498594	Total climb	300 ft (92m)
Map	Ordnance Survey Explorer Map: 1:25000 scale – Sheet 144		
Terrain	Village and country roads, grass footpaths, gravel farm tracks, woodland footpaths. There is a short section leading up to Nuthanger Farm which is a little awkward for pushchairs as it can get overgrown in summer months		
Obstacles	None		
Parking	This walks starts at The Royal Oak in Ecchinswell. Ecchinswell is 2 miles from Kingsclere. Head West out of Kingsclere on George Street and continue onto Newbury Road. After 0.2 miles turn left onto Fox's Lane, signed 'Fieldgate Centre', then after 0.1 miles, follow the road as it turns right onto Ecchinswell Road (passing a turning to Sydmonton on your left). Continue for 1.6 miles. At the junction in Ecchinswell turn left and The Royal Oak will be on your left		

The picturesque village of Ecchinswell was designated a Conservation Area in 1990 in recognition of the special architectural and historic interest of the village. The surrounding countryside is strongly undulating with fields enclosed within valleys, with the higher ground providing extensive views across the surrounding downland.

The route starts through the village, passing 'The Old School House' of Gothic design, which dates from 1861, built by the Kingsmill family of Sydmonton Court. Then crossing the village playing fields and along footpaths and country roads, the route passes through some beautiful countryside, including the rolling pastures of Watership Down Polo Yard. At this point there's an option to take a short cut along the road, back to the starting point, via the pretty village green.

The full walk continues up a fairly steep hill to Nuthanger Farm, as featured in Richard Adams classic book, Watership Down. Once at the top of the hill you're rewarded with far reaching views over the surrounding countryside and later over White Hill. The route continues down a lovely footpath under an avenue of trees to the final leg along a country road before reaching the village to walk alongside the river passing the idyllic Riverside Cottages.

Walk description

S. Leave the pub car park, turn right onto the road and continue straight on past a turning for Kingsclere on your right. After 130 yards, pass Mill Lane on your right and then continue past The Old School House and primary school buildings.

1. After 115 yards, turn left through a wooden fenced entrance into the village hall car park. Continue straight on across the car park, with a wooden slat fence on your left, to walk in front of the village hall and go through a large metal kissing gate at the end of the building. There's a play ground on your left as you enter the playing fields. Bear right to walk around the edge of the playing field, with a hedge on your right.

2. At the top right hand corner of the playing field, go through a gap in the hedge line, to follow a footpath around the right hand edge of an arable field. After 285 yards, in the corner of the field, continue straight on to follow a pretty footpath through Crowmarsh Copse. After 20 yards, pass a turning on your right and, after another 130 yards, pass a turning on your left.

   After 200 yards, the path emerges from the trees to run briefly along the edge of an arable field. Then after 75 yards, follow the footpath as it bears right back into trees. After another 60 yards, at the end of the path, walk around a log and then through a gap to the left of a wooden gate (take care as there's a ditch to the left).

3. Turn left onto the road and, after 120 yards, continue past Cowhouse Farm on your right. After another 215 yards follow the road as it bears slightly right, past a track on your left. Continue as the road climbs through trees.

4. After 300 yards, at a junction, cross the road to go through open wooden gates, entering 'Sydmonton Court Estate'. Follow the gravel track to the top of a hill and, after 125 yards, enjoy the lovely views across the valley.

   After another 120 yards, pass a grass track on your left. The arable field on your right is often sown to opium poppies which are grown under licence. The white and burgundy flowers present a spectacular sight in early summer months. Continue along the track as it gently descends over looking Watership Farm polo fields on your left. After 180 yards, continue down the hill passing a track on your right.

5. After 155 yards, pass a row of houses, known (but not signed) as 'Laundry Cottages' on your right. Then after another 200 yards, half way along the fairly straight section of track, turn left onto a gravel track alongside a polo playing field. Follow this track along the bottom of the valley towards Watership Polo Yard ahead.

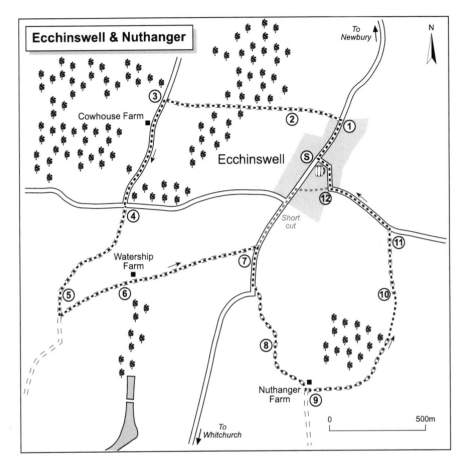

6. After 430 yards, turn right in front of the entrance to the polo yard. Then follow the track as it turns left around the stables and continue past Glasshanger Copse on your right. After 65 yards pass a small pond on your right. Follow the track with a hedge line on your left and horse paddocks on your right. Then after 265 yards pass a gravel track on your left.

7. After 400 yards, bear right at a fork and, in front of a house where there are often geese in the road, turn right onto a road (see below for a short cut from here). Then almost immediately cross over the road to join a grass track with sheep fields on your left. Continue along the grass track as it climbs gradually upwards and, after 245 yards, in front of an entrance to a field, bear slightly right join a narrow footpath that continues the climb up Nuthanger Hill. After 60 yards, push under a fallen tree then,

after another 55 yards, follow the footpath as it turns to the left. Take care along this section as the path can get over grown and is uneven in places.

8. After 205 yards, towards the top of the hill, go through an open gateway then, after 25 yards, with stables on your right, follow the path to the left of a second gate and along a fenced channel (or go through the gate if the path has become overgrown). Continue up the hill along a tarmac track. Then after 105 yards, as you pass a house (with a lovely outlook) on your right, follow the tarmac drive as it turns left. Continue along the drive, after 105 yards passing a barn on your left. After another 110 yards, follow the drive round to the right, as you pass the entrance to Nuthanger Farm on your left.

9. After 35 yards, turn left as indicated by the footpath sign, to follow a grass track around the left hand edge of an arable field. There are fantastic views over White Hill to your right and Isle Copse ahead. After 335 yards, at the corner of the field, continue straight on to follow a line of trees to your left, with a sheep field on your right. After 285 yards, follow the path as it bears left away from the field, then keep right to continue down the hill under a pretty avenue of trees.

10. After 245 yards, at the bottom of the hill, the path emerges from the trees to follow a grass track, pleasantly hedged on both sides.

11. After a further 350 yards, turn left onto Ecchinswell Road and follow this road back towards the village. Take care along this section as traffic can be fairly fast (walk on the outside of bends to increase your visibility to traffic).

12. After 460 yards, follow the road round to the right to walk alongside a stream. As you pass the gardens to the rear of the Royal Oak, look out for the witch's ducking stool that is still used each year on May Day, despite the stream only being six inches deep. After 100 yards, follow the road round to the left and over a bridge with white railings. Then after another 45 yards, at the junction turn left, then left again into the Royal Oak car park.

Short cut from point 7 (avoiding the climb to Nuthanger Farm)

At point 7 turn left to walk along the road back to the village. Follow the road for 335 yards, then continue past a turning on your left. After another 105 yards, just past White Hill (on your left), turn right signed 'Footpath'.

Follow the path under a large yew tree and continue to an open area of grass. There's an information board and wooden bench here, providing a stopping place for a picnic. Continue past a pond on your right to cross a footbridge and then, at the road, turn left to walk alongside the stream to join the full walk at point 12 above.

Refreshments

The Royal Oak
Hydes Platt, Ecchinswell, Newbury RG20 4UH
The Oak serves home-cooked bar meals. The lovely beer garden runs down to
the village stream.
www.royaloak-ecchinswell.co.uk

Local attractions

Sandham Memorial Chapel (3 miles)
Harts Lane, Burghclere, near Newbury RG20 9JT
A modest red-brick building housing an outstanding series of large paintings
by acclaimed artist Stanley Spencer. Inspired by his experiences as a First
World War medical soldier these paintings are considered to be among his
finest achievements.
www.nationaltrust.org.uk/main/w-sandhammemorialchapel

Krazy Klub (8 miles)
Newbury Leisure Park, Lower Way, Thatcham RG19 3AL
A soft play centre with a wide variety of custom designed equipment. Adults are
catered for with a variety of seating and good catering, with free parking.
www.krazy-klub.co.uk

Nuthanger Farm that featured in Richard Adams classic book 'Watership Down'

4. Nuthanger Down, Ladle Hill and Sydmonton

Distance	4.9 miles (7.9km)	Time taken	2 hours
Grade	★★★★★★	Postcode	SU491565
Grid Ref	RG28 7QH	Total climb	345 ft (105m)
Map	Ordnance Survey Explorer Map: 1:25000 scale – Sheet 144		
Terrain	Gravel farm tracks, footpaths across fields, woodland footpaths, short section of country road. The section leading down from Ladle Hill, below Wayfarer's Walk can get a little overgrown in summer months and muddy in winter months		
Obstacles	Soon after Sydmonton Court the route goes through a narrow gap to the left of a wooden gate. Extra care is needed as there's a ditch just to the left of the gap. We negotiated this obstacle by tipping the pushchair onto its right hand rear wheel and turning the left rear wheel over the ditch before pushing forwards through the gap. It is much safer with 2 people to guide the pushchair through this gap		
Parking	This walk starts from the top of Nuthanger Down, 3 miles south west of Kingsclere. Leave Kingsclere along Swan Street, B3051. After 0.3 miles, turn right onto Bear Hill, then after 165 yards, turn left onto Fox's Lane. Continue for 1.9 miles then turn left, towards Ashley Warren and Whitchurch. After 0.7 miles, as you emerge from trees at the top of a hill, park on the right hand side on the road, just after double metal gates		

This is a stunning walk, starting at Nuthanger Down to walk along Ladle Hill, which is a beautiful landscape of chalk escarpment, and part of the North Wessex Downs Area of Natural Beauty. The area is full of wildlife from buzzards and skylarks to a myriad of invertebrates feeding, in summer months, on the wealth of chalk land flowers. It's a visibly ancient landscape, indeed on top of Ladle Hill is a unique example of an 'unfinished' Iron Age hill-fort on the site of an earlier Bronze Age settlement. Evidence of its incomplete state, such as marking-out trenches, partly dug sections of ditch and untidy spoil heaps are apparent. Unfortunately, it's not open to the public.

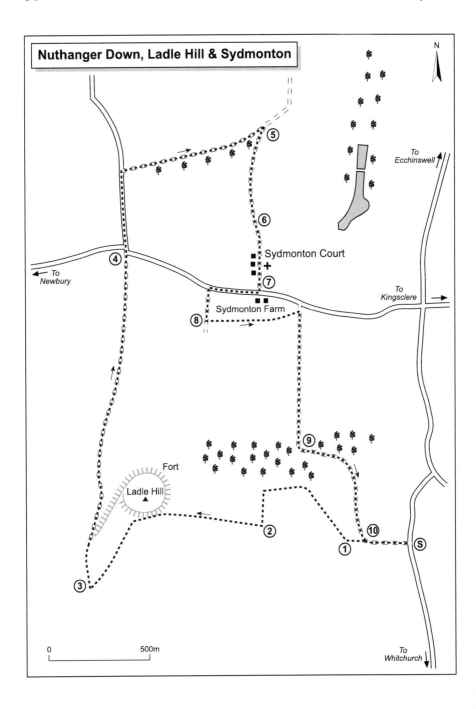

From Ladle Hill there are panoramic views across to Beacon Hill. Within the fortifications of Beacon Hill is the grave of the fifth Earl of Carnarvon who played a prominent part in the expedition to the 'Valley of the Kings' in Egypt, which led to the discovery of Tutankhamen's Tomb in 1922.

The route continues down a pretty woodland path, descending towards Sydmonton, then along gravel farm tracks to Sydmonton Court, with the neatly trimmed hedges of numerous horse paddocks. In the late 11th Century, Sydmonton formed part of the estates of Romsey Abbey. After the dissolution of the abbey, in the 16th Century, the manor of Sydmonton was granted to William Kingsmill and remained in the Kingsmill family until the 20th Century. Andrew Lloyd Webber, now Baron Lloyd-Webber of Sydmonton, bought the mansion and the 4,000-acre estate in 1978, and now keeps his Picasso and pre-Raphaelite art collection here.

The walk finishes on the pretty woodland footpaths though Baron Copse, then along the gently rising hill top, with impressive views over Nuthanger Down.

Walk Description

S. From the parking area, go through a small wooden gate to the right of double metal gates (or through a gap to the left of the double gates). Follow the gravel farm track with the line of large trees on your right. After 235 yards, continue straight on past a footpath gate and an electricity pylon on your right. After another 100 yards, nearing the end of the track, follow the track round to the right, then go through a small wooden gate (signed 'The Sydmonton Court Estate').

1. Follow a grass track across the field, parallel to the fence on your left. Continue along this path, then after 300 yards pass a small pond on your left, then bear left to walk past a small clump of trees and continue round the field. After 275 yards, at the end of the field, go through a small wooden gate, then immediately turn left to follow the field margin, with an arable field on your right.

2. After 175 yards, follow the grass track to turn right across the middle of the arable field. Then, after 150 yards, continue straight on past an earth mount on your left. After another 400 yards, pass a metal gate and a fence on our right and follow the grass track as it passes an Iron Age fort to your right. Then, after 175 yards, follow the track as it turns to the left and continues along the crest of the hill. At this high point of Ladle Hill, stop to admire the fantastic panoramic views, with Beacon Hill to the west.

3. After 435 yards, at a junction marked with a pile of flint rocks, turn right and follow the grass track down the hill to a metal gate 220 yards ahead.

Go through the gate and follow a pretty footpath through trees and on down the hill. After 950 yards, as you reach the bottom of the hill, continue along the footpath between trees. After another 125 yards, where the footpath becomes fairly flat, it can get muddy in winter months for the next 200 yards.

4. After another 245 yards, at the end of the footpath, cross over the road onto a minor road, signed 'Burghclere'. Then, after 265 yards, continue straight on past an entrance to Wergs Farm on your right, and after another 85 yards, immediately after Wergs Manor, turn right onto a gravel track, as indicated by a footpath finger post. Continue past New Wergs Cottages on your left and through an open metal gate. After 180 yards, continue straight on past a track leading to horse paddocks on your right. As you progress along this gravel track you'll have views ahead to a row of red brick cottages on the hill side, known as Laundry Cottages.

5. After 570 yards, follow the track round to the right and through a hedge line. Then immediately turn right onto another track. After 15 yards, continue through an open wooden gate. Then, after 110 yards, there are neatly trimmed hedges of horse paddocks to your right. After 300 yards,

The view from Ladle Hill looking across to Beacon Hill

pass a gravel track into a field on your left, then a black gate, also to your left. In springtime the field on your left is home to a flock of sheep with young lambs. After another 50 yards, continue through an open wooden gate into Sydmonton Court. This gate is monitored so that it will open well in advance of your arrival. If, in the unlikely event, it's still closed when you get to the gate you can press the button on the intercom to request that it is opened.

6. After another 50 yards, at a cross roads, continue straight on along a tarmac drive with ornate stone mushrooms on both sides. Continue past Sydmonton Court to your left, then after 135 yards, at a cross roads, continue straight on to pass red brick buildings with a central clock house on your right. Then keep straight to walk along a wood chip footpath alongside an avenue of trees.

7. After 175 yards, at the end of the path, go through the wooden gate to join a tarmac drive and continue down to the public road. Turn right and follow the quiet country road. Take care walking along this road as it's fairly narrow with poor visibility (walk on the outside of the bend to improve your visibility to oncoming traffic). After 285 yards, turn left to go through a gap to the left of double wooden gates. The gap is fairly narrow and there's a ditch to the left (obstacle). Once round the gate follow the grass track directly away from the gate, between hedges.

8. After 170 yards, turn left, down a shallow slope and through double wooden gates. Walk along the grass track between well kept hedges. Then after 150 yards, continue straight on to join a sand tack with wooden gates into paddocks on your right. After another 150 yards, keep straight on to join a gravel track with further paddocks to your right and an entrance to the estate buildings on your left. Continue straight on for another 190 yards to go through double wooden gates, which are usually open, then turn right on to another track. Follow this track toward Barton Copse and Nuthanger Down ahead. After 465 yards, pass entrances to fields on your left and continue along the track towards Barton Copse ahead.

9. After 105 yards, bear left at a fork in the track to continue along the footpath into Barton Copse, then after 155 yards go through a metal gate and continue up the hill though the woodland. After another 285 yards, follow the footpath as it emerges from the woods to continue straight on along a grass track.

10. After 415 yards pass a pylon on your right and continue up the slope to go through the small wooden gate at the top of the hill, then turn left onto the farm track to retrace your steps back to the road at the starting point.

Refreshments

The Royal Oak (2 miles)
Hydes Platt, Ecchinswell, Newbury RG20 4UH
The Oak serves home-cooked bar meals. The lovely beer garden runs down to the village stream.
www.royaloak-ecchinswell.co.uk

Local Attractions

Highclere Castle
Highclere Park, Newbury RG20 9RN (2 miles)
Highclere is one of England's most beautiful Victorian Castles set amidst 1,000 acres of spectacular Parkland. The Carnarvon family has lived at Highclere since 1679, although records show the Castle itself stands on the site of an earlier house, which in turn was built on the foundations of the medieval palace owned by the Bishops of Winchester. Open from Easter to Autumn.
www.highclerecastle.co.uk

The beautiful Victorian Highclere Castle

5. Bradley Wood

Distance	4 miles (6.4km)	Time taken	1 hour 30 mins
Grade	★★★	Postcode	RG28 7PW
Grid Ref	SU462514	Total climb	205 ft (62m)
Map	Ordnance Survey Explorer Map: 1:25000 scale – Sheet 144		
Terrain	Grass footpaths along field margins, woodland paths and tracks, a section of minor country road. A short section of the woodland tracks as you enter Bradley Wood can get quite rutted and a little muddy in winter months		
Obstacles	There is a narrow gap to go through at the start of this walk. If your pushchair doesn't fit through the gap it's advisable to take the pushchair through the gap straight from your car, before putting your child in the pushchair. Alternatively, if you arrive at the gate with your child already in your pushchair, follow the track along the fence line to the right of the metal gate, and then turn left onto a path partially blocked with logs. Immediately after the logs it's possible to cross the fence line, and then retrace your steps on the other side of the fence to return to the metal gate		
Parking	The walk starts 2 miles North of Whitchurch. Head North on Newbury Street, up the hill. After 1 mile, continue straight on past the turning for Kingsclere. Continue onto Larks Barrow Hill, and on past a turning on your right to Cole Henley. Then after another 0.2 miles, turn left onto a track (signed as a footpath). There's room for 3 or 4 cars to park along the side of the track before the bridge		

This walk starts fairly strenuously up a grass field margin adjacent to the A34, then continues alongside arable fields with views across the fields to woodland beyond, which in summer months contrast dramatically with a foreground of yellow rape. The route then continues along a pretty shaded footpath under an avenue of trees towards Cooper's-in-the-Wood Farm. Keep a look out for buzzards soaring overhead or glimpse a roe or fallow deer disappearing into the cover of trees.

The walk continues along a bridleway over undulating ground with far reaching views over open countryside. We have seen majestic red kite swooping amongst the mature trees along the hedge lines on this section. After nearly three quarters of a mile along a quiet country lane, passing Dunley Park, the route continues past Bradley Wood Farm and on into Bradley Wood. These woods are home to a diversity of wildlife, including many species of birds, mammals and invertebrates.

During spring months the woods bloom with a variety of spring flowers, most notable are the striking daffodils along the many of the woodland tracks.

Walk Description

S. Follow the gravel track under a bridge, crossing under the A34, and bear slightly left to a metal gate in front of you. Pass through a gap to the left of the gate (obstacle). Once through the gap, turn left and head up the grassy hill adjacent to the A34.

1. After 525 yards, in the corner of the field, continue straight on through a gap in a wide hedge line (20 yards across), then immediately turn right to follow the footpath adjacent to the hedge around the right hand edge of an arable field.

2. After 530 yards, at the next hedge line turn left around the corner of the field, and after a few yards turn right to cross the hedge line, then immediately turn right to continue along the grass footpath around the right hand edge of another arable field. After 85 yards, continue straight on under electricity cables. In the summer this field is a beautiful sea of yellow oil seed rape (not so good if you have a pollen allergy).

3. After another 365 yards, turn right at the bottom corner of the field to go past a short concrete pillar and then walk up a pretty avenue of trees. Continue straight on up a slope, after 205 yards, passing a grass field entrance on your right, and after another 95 yards, passing a grass track on your left. Then after 165 yards follow the track as it turns to the left.

4. After another 265 yards at the bottom of a slope, at a spacious junction, turn right to continue along an avenue of trees, passing a bridleway to your left. After 175 yards, continue straight on past a barn on your right, then after 40 yards, follow the grass path as it turns right and then left, with a hedge on your right.

   After another 245 yards, continue past a small wooded area on your left. Then after another 185 yards, at the end of the woodland, continue straight on up a gentle hill towards wooden gates ahead (the bridleway is actually to the right of the hedge but the field margin on the left hand side gives a smoother run for the pushchair).

5. After 250 yards, in front of double wooden gates, turn right and after 45 yards leave the field through a gap in the hedge, then turn right onto the road. After 125 yards, follow the road as it turns to the left in front of a wooded area, and to the right after another 35 yards. Then after 250 yards, continue straight on past entrance gates to Dunley Park.

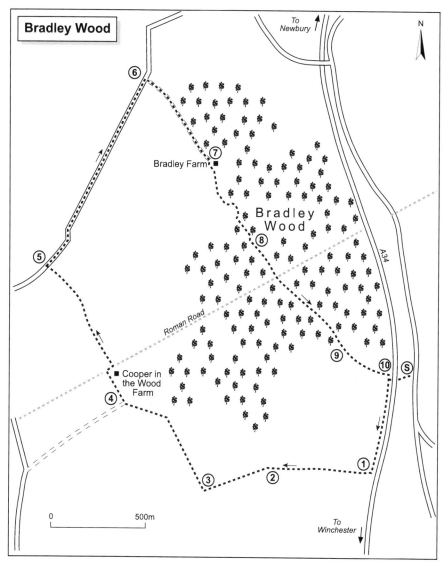

6. After another 800 yards, as the road bends left, turn right in front of wooden gates. Then, after another 440 yards, continue straight on along the road past a woodland entrance on your left, towards Bradley Wood Farm ahead.

7. After another 210 yards, pass a black round topped barn on your left, then immediately bear right to walk behind a stone barn. Continue around the barn

An avenue of trees through rolling arable landscape adjacent to Bradley Wood

to rejoin the track after 75 yards. Follow this track adjacent to the woods on your left. After 115 yards, as the track emerges to run alongside an arable field, bear slightly right to walk along the grass field margin to the right of the track.

Continue along the field margin alongside the track, then after 75 yards follow the grass margin round to the left, and after another 35 yards round to the right. Then after 80 yards, before the corner of the field, bear left to rejoin the track (just before a clearing to the left of the track). Follow the track with a wooded area on your right and the grass clearing on your left. After 100 yards, at the end of the clearing, follow the track as it turns slightly to the right.

8. After another 35 yards, bear left at a fork in the track to follow a grass track down through the woods. After 215 yards, continue straight past a grass track joining from the left, then after another 35 yards, keep straight on at a crossing of tracks. After 265 yards, continue straight on past a track to your left, then another after 180 yards and another after 60 yards.

9. After another 15 yards, as the track turns sharply to the right, continue straight on to follow a woodland footpath. Then after 50 yards, bear right where the path forks. Continue along this grass footpath, down a gently gradient towards the A34 ahead.

10. After 285 yards, at the end of the path, turn right onto a tarmac track and follow this under the bridge to the parking area at the starting point.

Refreshments

The Red House (2 miles)
21 London Street, Whitchurch RG28 7LH
The Red House welcomes children in the pub, restaurant and garden where there's a new kids play area. They have pub and children's menus or full à la carte is available.
www.theredhousewhitchurch.com

Local Attractions

Whitchurch Silk Mill (2.2 miles)
28 Winchester Street, Whitchurch RG28 7AL
The Silk Mill was built on the River Test in 1800, during the reign of King George III. This is a working water mill that produces high quality silks to order for theatrical costume, interior designers and historic houses. There's a duck pond, tea room (entry fee required) and a riverside garden which provides an ideal spot for a picnic.
www.whitchurchsilkmill.org.uk

Britain's only working Silk Mill in Whitchurch dates from 1800

6. St Mary Bourne and Swampton

Distance	2.5 miles (4km)	Time taken	1 hour
Grade	★★	Postcode	SP11 6BE
Grid Ref	SU421503	Total climb	170 ft (52m)
Map	Ordnance Survey Explorer Map: 1:25000 scale - Sheet 145		
Terrain	Level footpaths, farm tracks, minor country roads		
Obstacles	None		
Parking	St Mary Bourne is 4 miles North West of Whitchurch. Head West on Bell Street, and continue onto Bloswood Lane. After 1.3 miles continue onto Harroway and after 1.1 miles turn right at the B3048, signed to St Mary Bourne and 'Pick Your Own'. After 1.2 miles turn left to stay on the B3048. Turn right immediately after the The George Inn', then follow the road round to the left and over the bridge and immediately bare left onto Bourne Meadows. Turn right in front of the village shop to park		

St Mary Bourne parish is in an Area of Outstanding Natural Beauty and the villages of St Mary Bourne and Stoke form a Conservation Area. St Peter's Church is St Mary Bourne's oldest building, dating from around 1157, and has a very rare black marble font, which is at least 800 years old (and considered the finest in the country). The villages stand on the Bourne Rivulet, a chalk tributary of the River Test, and the upstream views from the Summerhaugh Bridge in the village square include buildings dating back to the 16th Century.

This walk starts at St Mary Bourne recreation ground, which has a children's play area, public conveniences and village shop. The route crosses the recreational ground then walks alongside St Mary Bourne's beautiful lake before climbing to higher ground to the south of the village, for great views over the village and surrounding countryside. The route continues through a wooded area which is home to a wide variety of wildlife. We've often seen deer casually foraging in the woods alongside the path near Derrydown Cottage. The walk proceeds along the hill top above the village, then follows a byway through trees back down into Swampton.

The final leg of the walk, from the primary school back to the recreation ground, follows the 'Walk to School Route' where old stiles have been replaced by locally crafted green metal gates each with an oval design depicting the shape of a Lollipop. Look out for the plaques displaying local children's poems on the five gate posts.

Walk Description

S. Walk around the village shop, keeping it on your right, passing recycling bins to go through a metal kissing gate and enter the village playing field. Follow the footpath straight ahead alongside a fence, passing St Mary Bourne lake on your left.

1. After 175 yards, at the top corner of the playing field, turn left through a metal kissing gate to follow a gravel path adjacent to the lake. After 265 yards go through another metal kissing gate, and continue on to a road 35 yards ahead.

2. At the junction, turn right to follow the road and, after 60 yards, keep right as the road forks, towards Derrydown House and Estate. Continue straight on up the hill and, after 245 yards, pass a footpath on your right.

3. After another 35 yards, follow the road as it bends to the right, then after another 50 yards, continue straight on past the entrance to Derrydown House. The field on the left is home to lambs in spring time. After 300 yards, continue straight on past Derrydown cottage (a bungalow) on your left. Then after 50 yards, go through a gap in the fence to the right of a black gate to continue straight on along a track adjacent to Derrydown Copse on your right.

4. After 200 yards, at the end of the Copse, at a crossing of tracks, turn right along a farm track. Continue along the track between hedges, then after 265 yards, at the end of the hedges, continue straight on at a crossing of paths to walk along the middle of a large arable field, with far reaching views to your right.

St Mary Bourne's beautiful lake

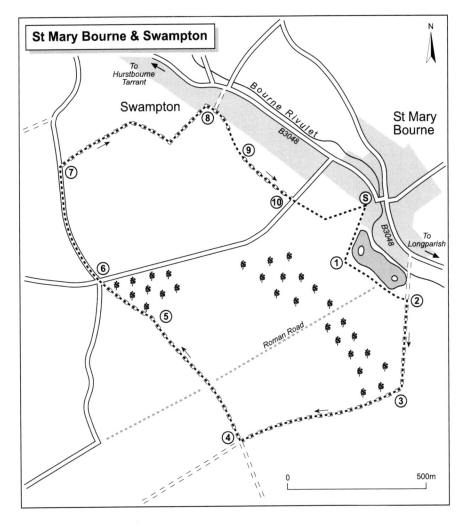

5. After 285 yards, continue along the track passing a house on your left, then after another 75 yards, pass green corrugated iron barns on your right. After a further 100 yards, continue straight on past a track on your left, and after another 45 yards, go around a black gate (or through it if it's open) to continue straight on along the farm track with Bedlam's Copse on your right (which is carpeted with bluebells in the spring).

6. After 75 yards, continue straight on at a cross roads, then immediately continue straight on at a second cross roads, towards Stoke (it's the only one

not sign posted, but is marked with a blue 'not suitable for HGVs' sign). After another 185 yards, continue straight on past a footpath in the hedge on your right and follow the road down a hill.

7. After 300 yards, towards the bottom of the hill and just before two wooden stables, turn right down a byway (marked with a small purple arrow). Follow this pretty path between trees towards Swampton. After 345 yards, follow the footpath as it turns to the right, passing a footpath on your left. Then, after 165 yards, follow the track as it turns to the left to go down a hill. After another 100 yards, continue straight on past a drive on your right, then after another 50 yards, pass a turning for the Test Way to your left.

8. After a further 35 yards, turn right in front of a primary school, onto a tarmac road. Continue past 'Gate Cottage' on your right and after a few yards past the entrance to 'Haven Hill'. Then, as the road

One of the 'Walk to school' initiative, locally crafted green Lollipop gates

bends to the left, bear right and, just past a wooden gate, go through the first of the Lollipop gates, signed 'Test Way'. Then follow a footpath across a grass field. After 85 yards go through another of these gates, and continue along the footpath across a second grass field.

9. After 100 yards, at the end of the field, go through another Lollipop gate and continue along the edge of an arable field along a gravel path.

10. After 300 yards, go through another Lollipop gate onto a road. Cross over the road bearing right to go through another Lollipop gate into a field. Follow the footpath across this field and, after 125 yards, go through the final Lollipop gate to enter to the village recreational field. Bear left to return to the car park at the starting point.

Refreshments

The Bourne Valley Inn
St Mary Bourne SP11 6BT
The Bourne Valley is a coaching Inn with a good reputation for freshly prepared food. They have a patio and large garden with has glorious views over a rambling stream.
www.bournevalleyinn.com

Local Attractions

Finkley Down Farm Park (4.5 miles)
Andover SP11 6NF
A family run children's farm with all the character of a traditional farm but in a safe environment. Visitors can feed the ducks and lambs, cuddle a rabbit or groom a pony. There's an adventure playground, trampolines, sandpit, tea room and plenty of picnic benches.
www.finkleydownfarm.co.uk

St Mary Bourne lake

7. Freefolk, Harrow Way and Bere Mill

Distance	4 miles (6.4km)	Time taken	1 hour 45 mins
Grade	★ ★ ★	Postcode	RG28 7PQ
Grid Ref	SU489483	Total climb	195 ft (59m)
Map	Ordnance Survey Explorer Map: 1:25000 scale – Sheet 145		
Terrain	Footpaths across grass and arable fields, woodland paths, minor roads. The walk is gently undulating throughout. The path across the arable field (at point 4) is sticky with mud during winter months. The footpath approaching Wells-in-the-Field Farm is a little awkward for pushchairs in a couple of short places as the path is fairly narrow		
Obstacles	None		
Parking	Freefolk is 1.5 miles from Whitchurch on the B3400/London Road. Continue into Freefolk, and then opposite Laverstoke Mill, turn right down Laverstoke Lane signed for Micheldever Station. Continue past a road side car park and sports club house on your right. Then just after a play ground, turn right into a small parking area in trees at Millennium Green. There are recycle bins here if you need them		

This walk starts at Laverstoke Millennium Green, which was created in 2000. The green comprises a children's play area, an adventure course and an area of woodland set against the adjacent parkland, through which this walk begins. Laverstoke grew up around the paper mill, which was founded in the 15th century. The existing mill building dating from 1719, used to supply paper for the Bank of England banknotes. Today the mill is not in use but may be converted for residential use.

After crossing parkland, the route continues through the ancient settlement of Freefolk, initially along the main road (using the pavement) with views to the left of the church of St Nicholas, which stands in a small field behind the rectory. This church is a small simple structure built in 1265 by William of Chabegrave, then owner of the manor, as a chapel to serve a small population. The church is worth a visit as it contains the tomb of Sir Richard Powlett, with a fine Jacobean monument, dated 1614. In addition, the royal coat of arms of King William III still hangs inside.

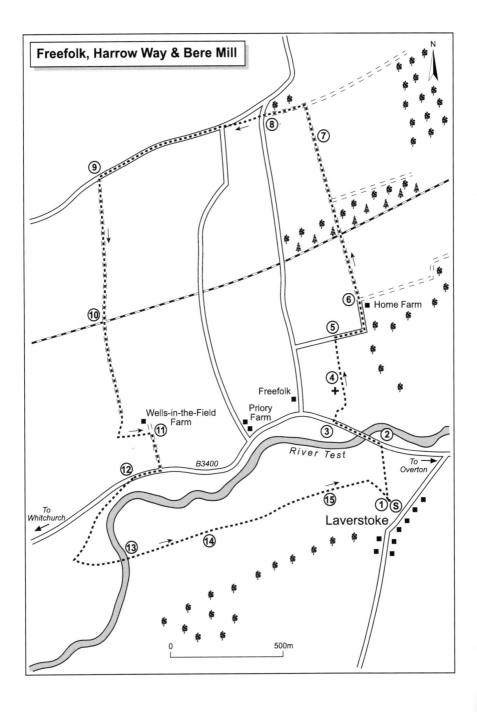

Freefolk, Harrow Way & Bere Mill

As the route turns off the B3400 it passes the end of a thatched terrace of eighteen estate workers cottages. The terrace was architect designed and is one of the longest, impressively thatched, buildings in England. The striking frontage contrasts with a rear view that is more utilitarian.

The walk then climbs gently to the Harroway which forms the western part of an ancient trackway dating from the Neolithic period. It can be traced from the Straits of Dover to the Devon coast, and is referred to as the 'oldest road in Britain' and may have been associated with ancient tin trading.

The final leg of this route passes the idyllic Bere Mill, now a private residence it was formerly a paper mill, owned from the early 18th Century by the Portal family. The walk continues through the fields beyond, which are home to a herd of Belted Galloway cattle, a rare breed of cattle originating from Galloway in South West Scotland.

Walk Description

S. Leave the car park heading away from the road, with a single storey tennis club house to your right. Walk into a field between a green wire fence and a line of large conifer trees. Continue along the row of conifer trees towards a sheep fence ahead. After 75 yards,

The idyllic Bere Mill was formerly a paper mill

at the end of the conifer trees, bear right to go through a small metal gate into a large pasture field.

1. Follow a grass footpath diagonally across the field, heading for some chimney pots under a lone conifer tree. After 100 yards, once you can see the house under the chimney pots (this is The Old Rectory), bear right and head down the slope to a gate to the right of the garden of the same house.

2. After 125 yards, at the bottom of the hill, go through a wooden kissing gate, to the right of a metal farm gate. Then turn left onto the road, crossing over to use the pavement. After 85 yards, continue over a bridge with white railings. Then, after another 85 yards, continue past the entrance to Laverstoke Park on your right.

3. After another 40 yards, turn right towards St. Mary's Church. Continue past the thatched houses on your left, and then bear right up a fairly steep hill towards the church. In front of Christmas Cottage, in line with the church gate, bear right to follow a path up three small steps (or dirt ramp to their right) and through a brick gateway. Follow the path as it turns left and into a wooded area (with a carpet of snow drops in early spring).

4. After 85 yards, continue straight on into an arable field, and follow a path directly across the field, in line with telephone cables. This field can get sticky with mud during winter months.

5. After 175 yards, at the end of the field, continue through the open gateway and turn right onto a single track country road. After 150 yards, follow the road as it turns left towards Overton Rugby Club. Then, after 65 yards, continue straight on past a farm entrance on your right. After another 100 yards, continue straight on past a red letter box on your left and a turning on your right.

6. After 135 yards, as the main track turns right to the rugby club, continue straight on to follow a farm track. After another 165 yards continue over a railway bridge, then after a further 145 yards, keep straight on at a crossing of farm tracks and on past a water tower after another 105 yards.

7. After 185 yards, continue down a slope, then after another 95 yards, turn left onto the Harrow Way. Within a few yards, where the track forks, take the main track to the left.

8. After 225 yards, continue straight on as the Harrow Way crosses a tarmac lane, 'Watch Lane'. Then, after 105 yards, turn left onto the road, and after another 30 yards, fork right past the top of Priory Lane to continue along the Harrow Way (now a tarmac road). After 250 yards, continue straight on past 'North Woolding House', following the road up a gentle slope. After another 200 yards continue down the other side of the hill.

9. Then, after 190 yards, on the downward slope, turn left onto a footpath (finger post on the right hand side of the road). Follow this footpath along a grass verge on the left hand edge of an arable field. After 365 yards, continue straight on past a hedge line to your right.

10. After another 245 yards, continue straight on over a railway bridge. After 450 yards, the path overlooks Wells-In-The-Field Farm to the left, then after another 125 yards follow the path as it turns to the left and continues down a slope.

11. After 140 yards, at the bottom of the hill, turn right onto the Wells-in-the-Field Farm drive and follow it for 195 yards down to the B3400. Cross over the road to use the pavement and turn right towards Whitchurch.

12. After 150 yards bear left off the pavement and down a short slope onto a footpath under trees. Follow this path straight on adjacent to a river to your left. After 480 yards, at the end of the path, in front of a wooden gate, turn left onto a tarmac drive. After 70 yards continue straight on over a small red brick bridge.

13. Then, after 200 yards, follow the drive over a larger red brick bridge across the River Test, with views over Bere Mill to your right. From the bridge bear left, turning off Bere Mill drive to go through a small wooden gate to the left of a metal farm gate, with two red brick houses to your left. Follow the grass footpath up a gradient, across a field and after 55 yards, go through a wooden kissing gate, and continue along a grass path across a much larger field.

14. After 335 yards, at the top of the field, go through another wooden kissing gate, crossing a line of large trees. Continue past a small metal bench and straight on along the top edge of an arable field, with a wire fence on your right.

After 375 yards, continue straight on over a short section of uneven ground with a cluster of trees to your left. After another 45 yards, continue straight on alongside a wire fence to you right.

15. Then, after 200 yards, with a house to your left, bear right up towards the fence line, past a track leading out of the field on your left. After

The Harrow Way which forms the western part of an ancient trackway dating from the Neolithic period

25 yards, in the corner of the field, go through a wooden kissing gate. Then immediately cross a farm track on a slight rightward diagonal to go through another wooden kissing gate (to the right of a gateway closed with a wire fence).

Follow a footpath directly across an open grass field to pass a large solitary conifer on your left after 100 yards. Continue straight on along the grass footpath, then after 85 yards, with a group of trees on your right, bear right towards a small metal gate next to tennis courts. After 70 yards go through the metal gate, then follow the footpath back along the row of conifer trees to the car park at the starting point.

Refreshments

The Watership Down (0.75 miles)
Freefolk Priors, Whitchurch RG28 7NJ
This pub has a large garden with picnic tables under trees, which is great for a drink after a walk. There are some chickens in this garden which the little ones love to watch. They have also recently got two piglets called Minty and Cheery which are kept adjacent to the garden.
www.watershipdowninn.info.

Local Attractions

Basingstoke Aquadrome (8.5 miles)
Leisure Park, Worthing Road, Basingstoke RG22 6PG
One of the largest flume attractions in the country. Enjoy a great family day out with three large flumes; rushing rapids, water features, spa pool and a baby beach. The Aquadrome also has a 25m competition pool where the keen swimmer will find lanes available.
www.basingstokeleisure.com/aquadrome/FAC_Pool

Milestones, Hampshire's living history museum (8.5 miles)
Leisure Park, Churchill Way West, Basingstoke RG23 6PG
Milestones is packed full of the things that ordinary people used in the past. It's is an ideal family visit with lots to explore in a safe, warm, child-friendly environment, all under one roof, including café, Edwardian-style pub and gift shop.
www3.hants.gov.uk/milestones

8. Whitchurch Mills

Distance	3.3 miles (5.3km)	Time taken	1 hour 15 mins
Grade	★★	Postcode	RG28 7AJ
Grid Ref	SU462478	Total climb	55 ft (17m)
Map	Ordnance Survey Explorer Map: 1:25000 scale – Sheet 144		
Terrain	Footpaths across fields on well established paths. The footpath after The Green is fenced off from the adjacent cow field and can get a little over grown in summer months, making it a little awkward with a pushchair. In winter months the cattle field after Bere Mill can get muddy, but it can be avoided by picking your path		
Obstacles	None		
Parking	Park at the Gill Nethercott Centre car park. From the mini roundabout in the centre of Whitchurch head South on Winchester Road for 225 yards, immediately after the Silk Mill, the Gill Nethercott Centre car park is on the right		

Whitchurch is an attractive town, first established as a borough in the 13th century. Due to its situation over the River Test, and being at a crossing of two important routes (Oxford to Southampton and Basingstoke to Salisbury), it became the first overnight stopping point out of London in coaching times. The original 'White Church' was probably built of chalk or limestone.

The small town once had a working mill located every half mile along the River Test, and is now home to Britain's only working silk mill. The mill building dates from 1800 and it's the only productive mill along the upper reaches of the River Test. This walk takes in three of the mills along the River Test, which is a clear chalkland river of great wildlife diversity. From the many footbridges you can see large brown trout that will compete with ducks for bread thrown into the water. The riversides are rich in wild flowers and provide a habitat valuable to birdlife.

At the furthest point of this circular walk you'll pass the attractive Bere Mill. Now a private house, Bere Mill was built in 1710 originally as a corn mill. Then in 1712 Henri Portal first established his paper making business here and, in 1724, won the contract to produce Bank of England notes. Henri Portal is buried at All Hallows church in Whitchurch. Further along the route you can view the Town Mill. A mill on this site was mentioned in the Doomsday Book and the current mill was still milling corn until 1940. After the war it fell into disrepair, until it was converted into a residence in 1969.

Walk Description

S. Leave the Gill Nethercott Centre onto Winchester Road and turn left to cross the river. After 65 yards, turn right down Test Road, in front of a florist, 'Flower Power'. Continue past allotments on your right and, after 215 yards, follow the road as it turns to the left. Continue to the end where Test Road joins London Street after another 135 yards.

1. Turn right onto London Road, then after 110 yards, turn right down Town Mill Lane. Follow this lane alongside the river and, after 120 yards, continue straight on past a metal railed footbridge on your left.

2. After another 110 yards at a gravel turning area, turn left up a narrow foot path just after the last house on your left. The path has a red brick wall on its left. Follow this path over a couple of wooden footbridges, then after 150 yards turn right onto Meadow Pound.

3. After 35 yards, at a junction, turn right onto The Green. Follow this road for 275 yards to its end, then continue straight on along a footpath between two hedges to a gate, 120 yards ahead.

4. Go through the small wooden gate to the left and continue along a footpath alongside a field which is often grazed by Belted Galloway Cattle.

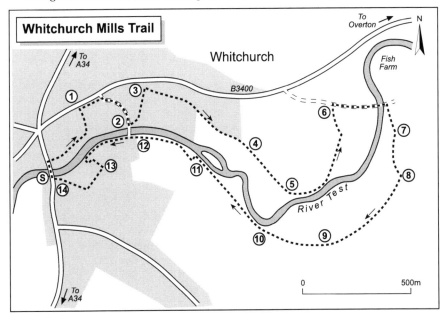

A fine old red brick bridge crossing the River Test at Bere Mill

5. After 325 yards, follow the path round to the left, up a small rise and then round to the right between two wooden gates. There's usually a flock of Black Welsh Mountain Sheep in the field to your left. After 240 yards you'll see the River Test through the trees on your right. After another 260 yards, follow the footpath as it turns to the left, then after another 60 yards go through a wooden kissing gate in the hedge line, and bear slightly left to cross a field on a diagonal to a wooden gate ahead.

6. After 260 yards, go through the kissing gate and turn right onto a tarmac drive towards Bere Mill. After 70 yards cross a small red brick bridge, then after another 200 yards, continue over a fine old red brick bridge, crossing the River Test. Then follow the drive around to the right towards Bere Mill. After 70 yards, as you approach the house, follow the track to the left, passing Bere Mill on your right.

7. After 155 yards, go through a wooden gate into a field. There are often more Belted Galloway Cattle in this and the next field so be careful to shut and latch all gates. Follow the fence line on your right, then after 100 yards, before the corner of the field and next to a wooden gate, turn left to follow the fence line up a slope to a smaller wooden footpath gate 55 yards ahead.

8. Turn right to go through this gate, then follow a path under a line of large trees along the length of a crescent shaped field. We have often seen red kite hunting above the meadows to the right of this field.

9. After 565 yards, towards the end of this long field, go past a metal gate on your left and continue straight on through a small wooden gate. Follow a footpath, which can get overgrown in summer months, along the fence line and on into a wooded section.

10. After 285 yards, go through a large metal kissing gate to follow a footpath along the right hand edge of an arable field, with the River Test through the trees on your right. After 225 yards continue straight on through a hedge line to walk along the right hand edge of another arable field.

11. Then, after a further 325 yards, in the corner of the field, bear left to follow the footpath away from the river, then after 15 yards turn right to go through the hedge line and enter Daniel Park. Continue straight on following the right hand edge of this field, with the primary school ahead to your left.

12. After 300 yards, continue straight on along the path as it enters a wooded area in the corner of the field below the school. After 65 yards you'll come to a small red brick arch over a black metal gate (through which you can see the

Belted Galloway Cows

water wheel of Town Mill). To see more of the Town Mill turn right in front of the gateway and after a few yards you'll reach a wooden footbridge in front of the mill. Here you'll find some large trout under the bridge that will make a splash, competing with the ducks for bread. There's often a pair of swans here too.

To continue on the walk retrace your steps back into the wooded area, with the red brick gateway on your right. Follow the path round to the right, passing a large lime tree on your left, then turn right in front of a small metal gate (an entrance to the primary school playing fields). Continue along the footpath alongside a wire fence, with the school playing fields on your left.

13. After 400 yards, follow the path as it turns right, away from the playing fields. Continue straight on to join McFauld Way and, after 90 yards, at the corner of a recreational field, turn right to follow a tarmac footpath down the side of the field. There's a playground to your left.

14. After 115 yards, at the bottom corner of the field, bear right and then immediately turn left to continue along a footpath with a stone wall on your right. After 75 yards cross Winchester Street and proceed straight on into the Gill Nethercott Centre car park at the starting point.

If you have any bread left and would like to feed more ducks, turn right just before you get to the parking area, to go through a small wooden gate into the Silk Mill grounds (closed on Mondays).

Refreshments

The Shop Next Door (0.1 miles)
5 Newbury Street, Whitchurch, Hampshire RG28 7DW
The Shop Next Door is a lovely little tea shop serving freshly ground coffee, teas, scrumptious home baked cakes, delicious soups, Panini's and baguettes.
www.glass-foolery.co.uk/#/tea-shop/4532188376

Local Attractions

Whitchurch Silk Mill (Start)
Whitchurch Silk Mill, 28 Winchester Street, Whitchurch, Hampshire RG28 7AL
The Silk Mill was built on the River Test in 1800, during the reign of King George III. This is a working water mill that produces high quality silks to order for theatrical costume, interior designers and historic houses. There's a duck pond, tea room (entry fee required) and a riverside garden.
www.whitchurchsilkmill.org.uk

9. Longparish Village

Distance	4.4 miles (7km)	Time taken	1 hour 30 mins
Grade	★★	Postcode	SP11 6PB
Grid Ref	SU426439	Total climb	105 ft (32m)
Map	Ordnance Survey Explorer Map 1:25000 scale – Sheet 144		
Terrain	The first section is on village and country roads and footpaths; the route then continues on good quality farm tracks. The final leg of the longer route gets muddy in winter months		
Obstacles	None		
Parking	Longparish is situated on the B3048, 1.3 miles north east of the A303, 6 miles East of Andover. Park in the gravel church car park accessed through the primary school car park, located at the Middleton end of the village		

Longparish is situated in the valley of the River Test and has a variety of wildlife rich habitats, including the river itself, water meadows, wetland scrub, chalk grassland and scrub, woodland and hedgerows. The village actually consists of a number of hamlets, including Forton, Middleton, Longparish Station, West and East Aston. Most of the village has been designated a conservation area, having around 80 listed building and monuments.

This walk starts in Middleton at St Nicholas Church, which dates from the early 13th century, and has a pretty 15th century tower of chequer flint and stone. The route follows country roads crossing branches of the River Test a number of times and before walking alongside a particularly picturesque section of river and passing Longparish Upper Mill. Built circa 1870 this mill was milling flour until about 1906, and then was used to supply electricity to Longparish House. Recently Rupert Dawnay restored the machinery, and it ran again in March 1998.

The route continues past East Aston House, with its stuccoed walls and six pointed Gothic casements, to join footpaths around arable fields, after which there's an option to take a short cut along the main village road back to the church. The full route continues along farm tracks, up a gentle gradient under an archway of mature trees, and then makes its way over undulating arable land on the north side of the village to return down Sugar Lane and past the Plough Inn to the start point.

Walk description

S. Leave the car park and turn right onto the road. After 50 yards continue past The Plough Inn, then after another 90 yards turn right onto Southside Road, signed 'Barton Stacey'.

1. After 150 yards cross the river and continue along this quiet country lane to cross a tributary of the river in 100 yards. After another 175 yards pass a 'no through road' on your left and continue past some houses. Then, after 220 yards, continue straight on past the top of Mill Lane.

2. Continue over another bridge, passing the entrance to 'Testwood Trout Fishery' then, immediately turn left onto Nuns Walk, just before 'Southside Farm House'. Continue along this single track road, and after 365 yards pass the entrance to 'Owls Lodge Farm' on the right. After another 85 yards, continue straight on past a turning on your left (which crosses the river by means of a deep ford).

3. After 650 yards pass Vale Farm on your right, then after another 75 yards, continue straight on past Vale Farm Fisheries to your left.

4. After a further 700 yards, at a junction, turn left onto a minor road opposite the entrance to Larkwhistle Farm on your right. After 100 yards follow the road round to the left to walk alongside a lovely chalk bed river.

5. After 140 yards, you have an option to take a little detour to a wooden footbridge over the river. It's a lovely spot so worth the extra few yards. To make the detour turn right onto a footpath, signed with a finger post. Follow the footpath over a short footbridge then continue to a much longer wooden footbridge. Take a few moments to enjoy the peaceful scene then retrace your steps back over the shorter footbridge to the road. Turn right onto the road to continue the walk.

6. After 350 yards cross the river over a bridge with white railings. On your right is a clear pool which maybe inviting on a hot summer

Longparish Upper Mill, built circa 1870 and was a working flour mill until about 1906

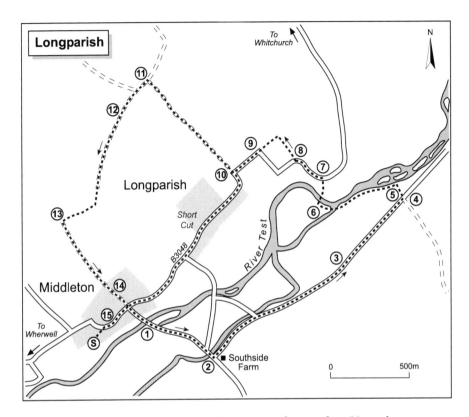

day, but swimming is not allowed. Continue for another 60 yards to cross a similar bridge, this time with the Mill House to your right.

7. After 35 yards follow the road round to the right and past 'Longparish Upper Mill' on your right. Continue to the end of the drive and turn left onto the main road into the village. Take great care along this section of road as it can be fairly busy. Walk on the outside of any bends to maximise your visibility to oncoming traffic.

8. After 265 yards, as the road turns to the left, next to East Aston House, turn right onto a gravel track, passing houses on your right. After 100 yards continue onto a grass track. Then, after another 100 yards, follow the track round to the left, and after 50 yards keep left to continue along the right hand edge of an arable field.

9. After 130 yards, just before the road, turn right and then immediately left to walk along the left hand edge of another arable field (this is a permissive path).

10. After 220 yards bear left to exit the field, then immediately turn right onto a restricted byway. There's a short cut directly back through the village from this point (see below). For the full route follow the grass track (which soon becomes a stone track) between two hedges up a gentle hill. After 700 yards, having reached the top of the hill, continue down a gentle slope.

11. Then, after 220 yards, turn left onto a gravel track with a grass verge down the middle. After 100 yards continue straight on past a grass track on your right and a strip of woodland on your left.

12. After another 155 yards, continue straight on past a footpath across an open field on your left (marked with a finger post to your right). After 265 yards, continue straight on past a grass track on your right and a large hedge on your left. Then, after another 455 yards, continue past a grass tack on your right, then a few yards further on past another grass track on your left. Continue along the gravel track, following it as it turns to the right.

13. Then, after 200 yards, pass a wooden finger post on your right and turn left onto a rutted grass track to continue along the Test Way (as indicated by the finger post) with a line of trees (large hedge) on your right. This track can get muddy in winter months making it very difficult for pushchairs. If the crop in the arable field on your left has been harvested it's easier to walk along the edge of the field alongside the track.

14. After 550 yards, pass a turning to your right and continue straight onto Sugar Lane. After another 235 yards, at a junction, turn right onto the main road though the village, signed 'Wherwell'.

15. After 85 yards pass The Plough Inn and cross over the road to use the pavement. After another 150 yards, turn left though the primary school car park and on to the church car park at the starting point.

Short Cut from point 10

This short cut avoids the potentially muddy section by following the main road though the village. Great care should be taken when walking along the road, especially around the bends as it can be fairly busy.

From point 10, instead of turning right onto the Restricted Byway, continue straight on to follow a footpath, with a post and rail fence on your left. After 190 yards, follow the path as it turns to the left and then, after a few yards, to the right. After a further 45 yards, at the end of the path, turn left onto North Acre road. Continue along the road and, after 55 yards, follow the road as it bends to the left, passing a turning to your right.

After 45 yards, at the end of the road, with the village shop on your left, turn right onto the main road through the village. Pass The Cricketers Inn on your left, then after 330 yards continue straight on past Mill Lane, signed to Barton Stacey. After another 45 yards continue past Longparish Cricket Club on your left (blue sign), then follow the road round to the left and on past a children's play ground.

Once you've extracted your children from the play ground, continue along the road, and after 75 yards passing 'Ash Burn Rest' (a pair of wooden seats) on your right. After another 280 yards, follow the road round to the left, then continue straight on at a cross roads (with Sugar Lane on your right and South Side Road on your left) to join the walk at point 15 above.

Refreshments

The Plough Inn
Longparish SP11 6PB
The Plough Inn dates back to 1721 and is on the Test Way making it an ideal watering hole for thirsty ramblers. A familiar sight at the inn is the webbed residents of Longparish who waddle over for a bite to eat from anyone who can bear to share their baguette! The Plough was sympathetically refurbished in late 2006 and has a warm and comfortable atmosphere, with flagstone and oak floors complimented by leather chairs and subtle soft furnishings, open log fires and superb food, wines and real ales.
www.theploughinn.info/

The Plough Inn in Longparish dates back to 1721

Local Attractions

Andover Museum (5 Miles)
6 Church Close, Andover SP10 1DP
Trace Andover's history from Saxon times to the present day. Step inside the Museum of the Iron Age and discover a way of life that was destroyed by the Romans.
www3.hants.gov.uk/andover-museum

Thatched cottage opposite the school at Longparish

10. Wherwell and Harewood Forest

Distance	5.1 miles (8.2km)	Time taken	2 hours
Grade	★★★★★	Postcode	SP11 7JH
Grid Ref	SU390408	Total climb	245 ft (75m)
Map	Ordnance Survey Explorer Map: 1:25000 scale – Sheet 131		
Terrain	Short section of village roads, then much of the walk is on the Test Way and forest tracks. There's a short section of uneven path in the forest. The first section of the walk is undulating and feels fairly strenuous but once in the forest the going becomes easier		
Obstacles	None		
Parking	Wherwell is situated 3 miles south east of Andover. From the A303, head south on the A3057. After 1 mile pass the turning to Goodworth Clatford and after another 0.3 miles turn left onto the B3420, Winchester Road. After 1.5 miles, continue into the village then, at the war memorial turn right onto Church Street. Just before the end turn left between red brick gate posts into the church car park		

This is a lovely walk through the picturesque Wherwell village and Harewood Forest. Wherwell is one of the most attractive villages in the Test Valley. There are many thatched and timber frame cottages lining the main road through the village, beautifully donned with spectacular flower displays through the spring and summer months.

Harewood Forest, just to the north of the village, is a former hunting ground of Saxon Kings. The forest is accessible via its many public rights of way, including a network of concrete tracks which were laid down during the Second World War when parts of the forest were used as ammunition dumps.

The walk starts in the church car park, originally a Saxon Church founded in AD 986, the present building is a mid-19th century gothic revival. The route proceeds up to the village High Street passing the war memorial, then leaves the village up New Barn Lane which has thick hedges providing a home to many types of bird, such as finches, tits, blackbird, thrush and jays. The fields above are planted with colourful yellow rape and blue flax, and as you enter the forest beyond you'll hear the cawing of rooks, jackdaws and crows in the trees above and you may catch a glimpse of deer retreating into the forest. In the spring you'll be greeted by a carpet of bluebells and primroses. As you continue through this ancient forest you may hear the eerie howling of the pack of bloodhounds kept at Park Farm. These hounds hunt the 'natural scent of man' to provide riders with a fun day out.

The route leaves the forest along the undulating paths on which the walk started, and two reasonable climbs later the route emerges back onto the High Street for another chance to take in the pretty thatched cottages.

Walk Description

S. From the church car park, turn right onto Church Street and continue to the war memorial at the end of the road. Then turn right onto the High Street passing a curving row of thatched cottages on your right. Continue along the pretty High Street and after 70 yards, pass the entrance to Wherwell Priory.

1. After another 45 yards turn left onto New Barn Lane. Then, after 100 yards, as the track double backs on itself, continue straight on up the hill, joining the Test Way. This path is a little stony on the uphill section. After 65 yards, continue straight on past a path leading up to a field on the right. Then, after 150 yards, the stones dissipate for a smoother ride. Continue for another 200 yards to the top of the hill, then follow this lovely shady footpath downhill.

2. After a further 270 yards, at the end of the footpath continue straight on, crossing a track diagonally, then follow a footpath to the right of a white

The war memorial stands in front of thatched and timber frame cottages of Wherwell village

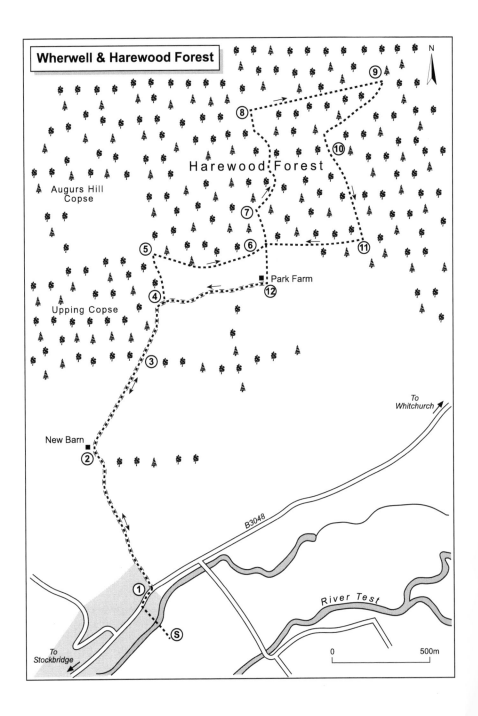

house, up a short but steep hill between trees. After 115 yards, continue straight on past an arable field on your left and on into Hassock Copse. After 275 yards there's a carpet of bluebells in early summer on your right as you approach the woods ahead.

3. After a further 45 yards, at the top of the slope, just before the larger woodland of 'Upping Copse', turn right onto a track, then within 20 yards fork left off the track to follow a footpath into the woods marked with a Test Way badge (ignore the first track in to woods to your left). Continue along the path adjacent to an arable field to your right. You can get a smoother ride along the edge of the field to the right of the footpath, but keep an eye on the footpath so that you can follow the directions. In the summer this field is often a beautiful sea of yellow oil seed rape flowers and in early summer there are more bluebells to your left.

4. After 100 yards, continue straight on over a grass track, then after another 200 yards follow the path round to the right. And after 35 yards, at a crossing of paths, turn left into the woods, leaving the arable field behind you, and passing a pit on your left. Continue down the hill on a fairly uneven footpath.

5. After 250 yards, at a crossing of tracks in a grass glade, turn right next to a footpath marker post. You'll see the remains of an enclosure on your right (also marked on OS maps). Follow this footpath along a woodland track. The first 100 yards of this track can get a little muddy in winter months. After another 420 yards, continue past the old fencing at the end of the enclosure and continue along the track, then after 50 yards bear left at a fork.

6. After 30 yards turn left onto a gravel track and, after another 40 yards, follow the track round to the left, passing a concrete track on your right. Then immediately take the right hand fork onto a concrete track, passing a forked track on your left. Continue northward along this concrete track towards Hartway Copse.

7. After 140 yards, pass a grass track on your right, then after another 25 yards take a right fork (there's a footpath marker post to the left just ahead of this turning). Continue up the hill along the concrete track and after 275 yards pass a grass track on your left, then after another 55 yards continue straight on past a gravel track on your left (which heads down to a pheasant enclosure).

8. After 295 yards, at a junction, turn right onto another concrete track, in front of a wooden finger post. After 125 yards continue straight on around double metal gates and then proceed straight across at a crossing of tracks. After 30 yards, step over a low slung chain (or around to the right) between six short concrete pillars. Then continue straight on along the track.

9. After 275 yards, keep straight on to join a concrete track and, after a further 225 yards, pass a grass path to the left. Then, after 45 yards, turn right in front of a footpath marker post (before a junction of tracks ahead). Follow the earth track as it bends round to the right (with another track joining from the left). After another 20 yards, continue straight on past a track on your left, along the track now with a grassy verge down the middle.

10. After 350 yards follow the track as it turns to the left. Then after a further 85 yards, next to a footpath marker post, continue straight on at a crossing of tracks into Beechen Copse. After 230 yards, keep right as the track forks. Then, after another 215 yards, pass two logs partially blocking the path and continue straight on to join another path.

11. After 75 yards (before a crossing of tracks 20 yards ahead), turn right towards a metal gate. Go around the gate to its left to access a concrete track, signed 'The Test Way'. After 300 yards, continue straight on past a field on your left. Then, after another 200 yards, at a crossing of tracks turn left onto a gravel track, signed Test Way. Follow this track as it curves to the left up a hill past a clearing on the right (at point 6).

Chilbolton Cow Common is a Site of Special Scientific Interest in the valley of the River Test

12. After 200 yards, at the top of the hill, pass Park Farm on your right, then immediately after the last concrete building, turn right down a farm track, signed Test Way. You may hear the bloodhounds howling as you pass. After 150 yards, at a junction of tracks (with a finger post on your left), continue straight on to follow the path with trees on your right and an arable field on your left. You can get a smoother ride along the edge of the field to the left of the path.

After 425 yards, continue straight on past the top of a footpath (at point 4) and continue on along the footpath following the edge of the Copse to your right and the arable field to your left. After another 370 yards, at the corner of the field (at point 3), cross the track on a long diagonal, then bare left to join a footpath back towards New Barn. Follow the path uphill and after 300 yards continue downhill. At this point I usually think I'm on the final stretch before realising there's another hill after New Barn.

After another 200 yards, at the bottom of the hill (at point 2), continue past the white house on your right, and cross over the track on a leftward diagonal, then bare right to follow a footpath into the trees and up the hill. After 250 yards at the top of a fairly steep hill, continue down the hill towards Wherwell. After 400 yards, where the footpath meets a track, take the left fork to follow the track down a slight gradient to its end. At the road turn right onto the High Street.

Continue back past the entrance to Wherwell Priory then turn left down Church Street in front of the war memorial. Just before the end of the road turn left into the car park at the start point.

Refreshments

The White Lion
Winchester Road, Wherwell SP11 7JF
A warm greeting awaits you at The White Lion Inn, nestling at the centre of the historic and picturesque village of Wherwell. They're family and dog friendly and welcome wiped muddy boots, children off the leash and dogs on.
www.thewhitelionwherwell.co.uk

Local Attractions

Chilbolton Cow Common
Fullerton Road, Wherwell SP11 7JT
Chilbolton Cow Common is a Site of Special Scientific Interest (SSSI) in the valley of the River Test. It's a great place for nature lovers, but also a fantastic place for a family walk or picnic. There's loads of space to explore and it is one of the few places where the clear chalk river is accessible to the public.
www.chilbolton.com/chilbolton-cow-common.htm

11. Goodworth Clatford and Harewood Forest

Distance	4.7 miles (7.6 km)	Time taken	2 hours 15 mins
Grade	★★★★	Postcode	SP11 7HL
Grid Ref	SU365425	Total climb	250 ft (76m)
Map	Ordnance Survey Explorer Map: 1:25000 scale – Sheet 131		
Terrain	Country road, bridleways, woodland footpaths and tracks. There are short sections of track in Harewood Forest that can get muddy in winter months		
Obstacles	None		
Parking	Goodworth Clatford is 2 miles south of Andover. From the A303, take the A3057/Winchester Road southwards, signed Stockbridge. After 1 mile turn right onto Church Lane. Continue past St Peters Close on the right, then immediately after the church turn right into the church car park		

This walk starts at St Peter's Church in Goodworth Clatford which began as a small nave and chancel, with further additions in the late 12th century. It has a 14th century tower and bells dating from 1622. The Anglo-Saxon derivation of Goodworth is believed to be 'Goda's enclosure' although little is known about Goda, and Clatford means 'the ford where the burdock grows'.

The route sets out away from the village to follow a bridleway across The Hampshire Golf Course and a farm track to join a footpath which crosses undulating farmland to reach Harewood Forest. Harewood Forest covers 670 hectares of mainly ancient semi-natural woodland and supports a distinctive flora and fauna. It's carefully managed and was recorded as a Countryside Heritage Area in 1989. Indeed it's the county's largest area of ancient woodland outside of the New Forest.

Harewood Forest is thought to be a remnant of the ancient Savernake Forest, one of the Royal Forests in late Saxon times. All hunting rights were reserved to the King and any felling was strictly regulated. These Forest Laws were reinforced until the *Charta de Foresta* of 1217. Within the forest are the remains of a railway line which operated until 1956 and concrete roads laid during the Second World War, when the forest was used to store munitions.

On the return trip this route follows the northern edge of Upping Copse, passing the keepers cottage where numerous pheasants are reared, then along a pretty footpath where, in spring time, the bluebells carpet the forest floor. Keep a look out for the bright plumage of green woodpeckers in these woods. The route finishes along the bridleway on which it started, across the golf course and back to the church at the starting point.

Walk Description

S. Leave the church car park and turn left on to Church Lane. Follow this road for 300 yards to a junction with the A3057. Cross this road with great care as traffic can be quite fast along this stretch.

1. Once across the road, continue straight on past a metal gate, then cross a grass track, passing another metal gate, to follow a bridleway. The golf course crosses the bridleway several times as you proceed along the path but continue straight on until you reach a farm track.

2. After 700 yards, at the end of the golf course, with a footpath marker on your left, turn left onto a farm track and follow it down a hill, in line with telephone lines above.

3. After 340 yards, at the bottom of the hill, just before twin telegraph poles, turn right to go through a gap in the hedge line. Negotiate a log partially blocking the gap, then follow the footpath along the left hand edge of an arable field. After 300 yards walk under electricity cables and continue up a fairly steep hill to a small copse ahead. Depending on the time of year you can get a smoother ride if you push up the hill to the right of the path using the tractor tracks.

4. After a further 340 yards, at the top of the hill, turn left through the hedge line. Then immediately turn right off the track to follow the path around the edge of a Copse. After 175 yards, continue straight on through a hedge line, passing a footpath marker post, then immediately turn right to continue along the footpath around the Copse. After 45 yards follow the path as it turns to the left, then to the right after a similar distance and back left after another 45 yards.

5. Continue along the footpath, leaving the copse behind you, to follow the field margin adjacent to a hedge on your right. Then, after 85 yards, turn right through a small open wooden gate and immediately bear left to follow a single file path through trees.

6. After 365 yards, at the top of a slope, join a track from your right to continue straight on into Furzy Croft Copse. After 100 yards continue between two corrugated metal domed sheds, and after another 25 yards continue straight on at a crossing of tracks. Then, after 35 yards, continue straight on past a

track on your right, then immediately past another on your left. Continue along a concrete track through conifer trees and after 200 yards, keep straight on past a track to the right.

7. After another 200 yards, at the bottom of a short slope, opposite a corrugated iron enclosure, turn right down a concrete track. Then after 30 yards keep left to stay on the concrete track, passing a grass track on your right. Continue along the concrete track as it sweeps through Hartway Copse. This is a lovely deciduous woodland which is especially spectacular in autumn leaf.

   After 865 yards, continue straight on past a forked footpath on your left (with a signpost to the right), and after another 40 yards continue past a grass track on your left.

8. After 125 yards, continue straight on past a forked track on the right, then follow the track round to the right, passing another track on your left. Continue along the track and, after another 40 yards, as the gravel track turns left up a hill, turn right onto a grass track (which is a little indistinct to start). Follow the grass track into Park Brow Copse, and after 85 yards pass the remains of an enclosure on your right (also marked on OS maps). Continue along the woodland track, which can get a little muddy for a short section towards the end in winter months.

9. After 550 yards, pass more old fencing at the end of the enclosure, then at a crossing of paths keep straight on, next to a footpath marker post on your

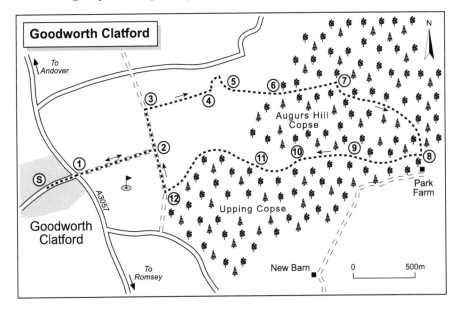

The 12th century St Peter's Church in Goodworth Clatford

left. After 40 yards, continue straight on at a crossing of tracks to cross a wide grass margin.

After 190 yards, where the track splits, follow the footpath by taking the right hand fork (this side seems to be smoother).

10. After 230 yards, turn left onto a concrete track and then after 30 yards follow the concrete track around the left hand edge of a large field. (It is possible to continue straight across the middle of the field on a grass track but there is no right of way directly across the field).

11. After 300 yards, before the concrete track turns left away from the field, bear right onto a grass track, to continue along the left hand edge of the field. After another 315 yards, towards the end of the narrow part of the field, you'll pass the 'Keepers Cottage' to your left. As you come level with the cottage, in front of a spear of woodland, keep left with the woodland on your right. Then, after 15 yards, turn right onto a footpath through trees. After 10 yards you'll pass a telegraph pole on your right.

After another 140 yards, continue along the footpath as it emerges from the trees to walk along the outside edge of the wood. Then after 50 yards follow the footpath as it re-enters the woods. Continue along this footpath along the edge of the woodland. In spring time there's a carpet of bluebells on your left.

12. After 700 yards, turn right onto a track with a footpath marker post on your right. Follow the track down the hill with the golf course through the hedge on your left. After 35 yards pass an electricity pylon on your left.

After another 385 yards turn left (at point 2), to retrace your steps down the bridleway, through the middle of the golf course. After 700 yards, continue straight on to cross a grass track, passing two metal gates (at point 1). At the road, cross over with extreme care (it's more difficult to see oncoming traffic from this side), onto Church Lane. Follow this road towards the village, and after 300 yards, just after the church, turn right into the church car park at the start point.

Refreshments

The Royal Oak
Village Street, Goodworth Clatford SP11 7QY
The Royal Oak is a country pub in one of the Test Valley's prettiest villages and provides a high standard of food, drink and real ales. They have a large well tended beer garden that attracts tourists, walkers and ramblers.
www.royaloak.me.uk

Local Attractions

Andover Museum (5 Miles)
6 Church Close, Andover SP10 1DP
Trace Andover's history from Saxon times to the present day. Step inside the Museum of the Iron Age and discover a way of life that was destroyed by the Romans.
www3.hants.gov.uk/andover-museum

Finkley Down Farm Park (4.5 miles)
Andover SP11 6NF
A family run children's farm with all the character of a traditional farm but in a safe environment. Visitors can feed the ducks and lambs, cuddle a rabbit or groom a pony. There's an adventure playground, trampolines, sandpit, tea room and plenty of picnic benches.
www.finkleydownfarm.co.uk

12. Abbotts Ann Village and Farm Tracks

Distance	4.1 miles (6.6km)	Time taken	1 hour 30 mins
Grade	★★	Postcode	SP11 7NP
Grid Ref	SU331435	Total climb	115 ft (35m)
Map	Ordnance Survey Explorer Map: 1:25000 scale - Sheet 145		
Terrain	Woodland and grass footpaths, gravel tracks, short sections crossing country roads		
Obstacles	None		
Parking	Abbotts Ann is 1.5 miles from the A303, just south of Andover. From the A303, take the A343/Salisbury Road, signed Middle Wallop and Grateley. Continue straight on at a minor roundabout to continue on the A343. Then after 0.3 miles turn right in front of Popular Farm Pub onto Little Ann Lane signed to Little Ann. Follow the road round to the right into Abbotts Ann and continue through the village and onto Church Lane. Opposite the church and immediately past a bus stop, turn left into the church car park		

Abbotts Ann is a pretty village set in the Test Valley, with its share of timber framed and thatched cottages. The village has a rural atmosphere of quiet tranquillity. The name formally 'Anne Abbatis' is derived from the original Celtic river name Anne, meaning 'Ash Tree Stream' (now known as Pillhill Brook), and that the land was granted to the Abbey of Hyde before the Norman invasion. During Roman times a large Villa was built at the end of Dunkirt Lane, mosaics from which are now in the British Museum.

In 1806, Robert Tasker settled in Abbotts Ann and became an assistant to a blacksmith, taking over the business in 1809. Here Robert Tasker and his younger brother, William developed the first iron plough, which became so popular they relocated a little way east, to the Waterloo Iron Works in Anna Valley, to cope with the demand. In 1831, Robert Tasker built the school on its present site in Abbotts Ann.

The walk starts along Church Path, passing two friendly donkeys, who will be happy to relieve you of any carrots you may be carrying. The walk continues past St Mary's Church, famous for its box pews and 49 virgin crowns. Church Path runs alongside church meadows with its majestic lime trees, including England's largest

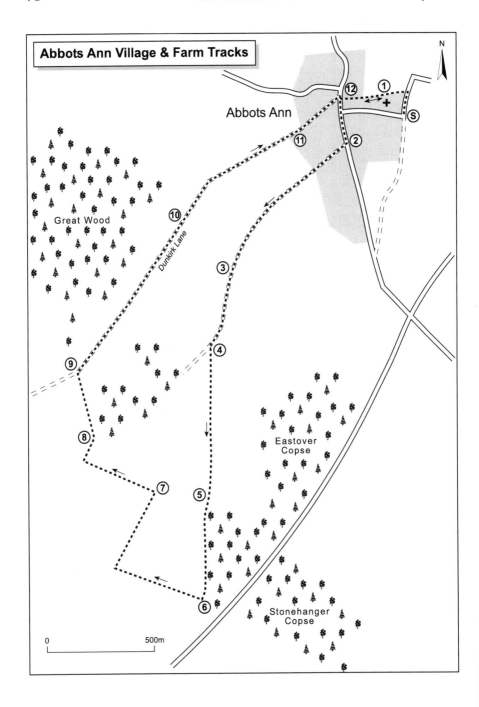

lime tree. On reaching the village centre, the route heads southwards along Red Rice Road before following The Drove past Bulbery Sports Ground and along a pretty footpath shaded by an arch of trees. The next section of the walk is on grass footpaths around arable land interspersed with woodland and coppices, home most notably to brown hare, deer and buzzards.

At its furthest point the route reaches Abbotts Ann Down before turning for home and continuing along grass verges around the edge of arable fields. The final leg of the walk joins a long gravel farm track known as Dunkirt Lane, which leads down to the Jubilee Oak and the village centre. Passing the village shop, the route finishes along Church Path back past the donkeys to the starting point.

Walk Description

S. From the church car park, turn right onto the road and cross over in front of the church. Turn left down a Church Path passing a donkey field on your right.

1. Follow the path passing the church on your left, with the church meadows to your right. After 230 yards, continue straight on through black railings, then after another 150 yards pass the village shop on your right. At the road, turn left and cross over to use the pavement. Follow the road, past The Eagle pub and then Church Road, both to your left, and continue straight on up the hill.

2. After 210 yards, with the crest of the hill in sight, turn right onto Webbs Lane leading to The Drove. Follow the road to its end after 150 yards, then continue straight on to join a footpath, passing steps and a drive on your left. After another 50 yards continue straight on past a footpath up a slope on your left (there's a playground in the field at the top of this slope). Continue straight on between logs, which partially block the path, to follow a pretty footpath beneath an arch of trees.

3. After 650 yards, at a junction with a farm track, continue straight on to join the track. Then, after 90 yards, as the track turns to the left, continue straight on to follow the footpath through trees.

4. After 380 yards (15 yards before a stile ahead), bear left at a fork to go through a hedge line. Then immediately turn right to walk a few yards along the edge of an arable field. Continue straight on to join a grass footpath across an open arable field. After 465 yards, at a crossing of paths, continue straight on through a hedge line, then bear left to follow a footpath along the left hand edge of an arable field.

5. After 205 yards, continue straight on past a track on your left, now with Cossical Copse on your left. After a further 45 yards, continue straight on past

a grass track to your left. Then after 220 yards continue past another grass track to your left.

6. After 255 yards, at the corner of the field, go through the hedge line and immediately turn right, (next to a footpath marker post) to follow a footpath along the edge of a wooded area to your right. After 455 yards, at the end of the wood turn right and continue along the path. After another 25 yards, continue straight on past a hedge line on your left.

7. After 415 yards, in the corner of the field, turn left to continue along the footpath, as indicated by the footpath marker post (and the private signs in all other directions). After 405 yards, follow the path as it turns right, heading towards the trees ahead.

8. Then, after another 125 yards, bear left some way in front of a Copse (The Groves) and continue along the path for 310 yards to a junction of farm tracks just past a Dunkirt Barn.

9. Turn right immediately past Dunkirt Barn to join Dunkirt Lane. Follow this track back towards the village. After 450 yards, keep straight on past a hedge line on your left and a small cluster of trees on your right.

The friendly donkeys at church meadow alongside St Mary's Church

10. After 465 yards, with a house to your left, continue straight on past a turning on the left. Then, after 45 yards, continue straight on past a turning on your right.

11. Follow the gravel track for another 700 yards, then go through a metal gate (or round it to the left). Then after another 145 yards, continue straight on along a residential street as you proceed back into the village.

12. After another 200 yards, at the end of Dunkirt Lane, turn right onto a pavement (passing an oak tree in the middle of the road to your left). Then after a few yards cross over Duck Street, bearing right towards the village shop. Immediately after the shop, turn left to follow a footpath past the church, retracing your steps back past the donkey field to the road. Turn right onto the road and after a few yards turn left into the church car park at the start point.

Refreshments

The Poplar Farm (0.5 miles)
Old Salisbury Road, Abbotts Ann SP11 7NJ
This pub offers traditional hospitality, freshly prepared pub food and lovely gardens alongside a pretty stream.
www.vintageinn.co.uk/thepoplarfarmabbottsann

Local Attractions

The Hawk Conservancy (3 miles)
Sarson Lane, Weyhill, Andover SP11 8DY
The Hawk Conservancy Trust is a conservation charity and visitor attraction. It's set in 22 acres of woodland and wild flower meadow, with over 150 birds of prey on view, from the tiny Pygmy Owl to the impressive European Griffin Vulture.
   Allow at least half a day for your visit as there is much to see and do. Visitors are offered three daily flying demonstrations that enable the participants to get closer to the birds.
www.hawk-conservancy.org

Museum of Army Flying (3.5 miles)
Middle Wallop, Stockbridge SO20 8DY
The Museum of Army Flying is home to a unique collection of aviation history, one of both international and national importance. There are over 35 historic fixed and rotary wing aircraft on display, that along with detailed dioramas, artefacts, trophies and models serve as an inspiring tribute to men and their machines.
www.armyflying.com

13. Stockbridge and Horsebridge on the Test Way

Distance	3 miles (4.8km) each way	Time taken	1 hour 20 mins
Grade	★	Postcode	SO20 6JA
Grid Ref	SU357346	Total climb	35 ft (11m)
Map	Ordnance Survey Explorer Map: 1:25000 scale – Sheet 131		
Terrain	Woodland and riverside footpath, gravel track. The route follows the Test Way along the river and is easy going with no hills		
Obstacles	None		
Parking	Stockbridge is 6 miles south of Andover. Take the A3057 southward, then after 3.4 miles turn right in Leckford. After another 2.6 miles, at a roundabout, take the second exit onto the A30. After 0.3 miles at a larger roundabout (almost in Stockbridge itself) take the first exit onto the A3057, then within a few yards turn right to stay on the A3057, signed Kings Somborne and Romsey. Pass Old St Peter's Church on your right, then immediately turn right onto a minor road, signed Marshcourt. After 0.2 miles continue past 'The Milsons' (with a large yew tree in front of a collection of bungalows) then turn right into 'The National Trust' car park. If you are driving to Horsebridge, it's 4 miles south of Stockbridge. Follow the A3057 southward and after 2.7 miles continue through Kings Somborne onto Romsey Road. After 0.6 miles turn right onto Horsebridge Road, then after another 0.6 miles turn right, signed Houghton. After a few yards, opposite the John O'Gaunt Inn, turn left, signed 'Test Way Car Park'. The car park is then on the right		

Stockbridge is a beautiful old country town with a collection of interesting shops, tearooms and inns along the broad High Street. It developed from a Saxon stronghold to defend against the Danes, then a prosperous market town attracting sheep drovers on their travels, to become a fishing capital, home to the oldest fishing club in the world. At the eastern end of the town is situated Old Peter's Church, a 12th century church featuring a medieval oak door and 16th century murals. This church is worth a visit in springtime for its lovely display of wild flowers.

The walk starts from The National Trust car park at the entrance to the Stockbridge Marsh Common, which is an ancient common, ecologically important for its diverse flora. The Common is grazed by cattle and horses and is a great place for a stroll along the Test River. This route doesn't enter the common but follows the Test Way initially adjacent to the common, then on past the towering chimneys of Marsh Court House. The route continues between thick hedges which provide a wonderful habitat for many species of birds, and then crosses The Clarendon Way (a 24 mile walk joining the two Wessex cities of Winchester and Salisbury).

The route continues alongside and over Park Stream, a branch of the Test which flows through John of Gaunt's Deer Park, which was created by William Briwere in the 12th century. The route then arrives in Horsebridge at a renovated Victorian railway station; a private residence open on selected weekends for afternoon tea. The station is beautifully preserved, complete with signal box, waiting room and a third class carriage.

Horsebridge is a tiny hamlet, on the River Test at the point where the original Roman road from Winchester to Sarum crossed the river. Other than the restored station the settlement comprises The John O'Gaunt Inn, which is popular with walkers, a large converted mill which is a grade II listed building and a few houses.

We have walked this route there and back, taking afternoon tea at Horsebridge station, allowing the little ones to have a run about and stretch their legs before heading back. Alternatively the route can be walked just one way, if you can arrange transport from either end.

Walk Description

From Stockbridge to Horsebridge

S. From the parking area, go through a small wooden gate towards The National Trust Marsh Common (Stockbridge Common). In front of a second gate, turn left onto the Test Way to walk along a pretty shaded path, with the common through trees to your right. After 880 yards you'll be able to glimpse Marsh Court House, with its towering chimneys to your left.

1. After another 350 yards, continue straight on past a small wooden gate which leads into Marsh Common. As you continue along the path keep a look out for Marsh Court Lake to your right.

2. After 1.14 miles, go through a gap next to a wooden barrier and continue straight on to join a gravel track.

3. After 285 yards, pass through a gateway to cross a gravel track (the Clarendon Way). Then continue through a second gateway to continue along the Test Way.

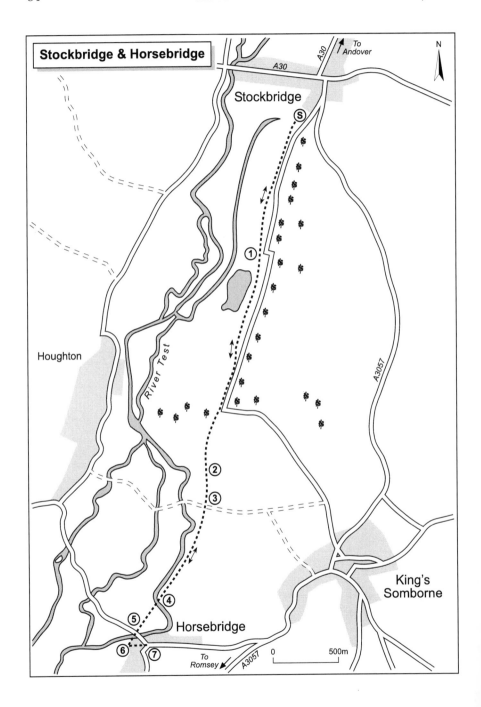

4. After 935 yards, follow the footpath over a large wooden bridge crossing 'Park Stream'.

5. After another 365 yards, continue up a ramp to cross a tarmac road and to continue along the Test Way on the other side of the road. Continue down another ramp and immediately over another long wooden bridge.

6. After 45 yards, cross a shorter wooden bridge, then immediately turn left at a crossing of paths (in front of a hedge and railway signal post). Follow the path round to the left, and then go through a gap in the fence to join a gravel track.

7. At this point you can turn right to have tea at the restored Victorian 'Horsebridge Station', or continue straight on, to the Test Way car park on your left. The John of Gaunt pub is straight ahead, at the end of this road.

From Horsebridge to Stockbridge

7. From the Test Way car park main entrance turn right onto the gravel track. At the end of the track bear slightly right to go through a gap in the fence to the right of the entrance to Horsebridge Station.

6. Follow a footpath round to the right. After 35 yards, at a crossing of paths turn right onto the Test Way and continue over a short wooden bridge. After another 45 yards, continue over a longer wooden bridge crossing 'Park Stream'.

5. Continue up a ramp to cross the road. On the other side of the road, continue down another ramp and along the Test Way.

4. After 365 yards, follow the footpath over a large wooden bridge,

3. Then, after another 935 yards, continue straight over a gravel track (the Clarendon Way).

2. After 285 yards, bear right off the gravel track to go through a gap next to a wooden barrier and continue along the Test Way.

1. After 1.14 miles, continue straight on past a wooden gate into Marsh Common on your left.

S Then, after 0.7 miles, next to the main entrance into Marsh Common, turn right into the parking area at the starting point.

Refreshments

The Vine Inn
High Street, Stockbridge SO20 6HF
The Vine Inn has a cosy restaurant with roaring log fires when the weather gets cold. Fresh homemade meals are served. There's a large, delightful garden with a branch of the Test River, stocked with fish, running through it. The fresh atmosphere keeps the garden cool on hot summer days and the sound of water gurgling is both pleasant and relaxing.
www.vine-inn-stockbridge.com

Local Attractions

Horsebridge Station (on route)
Horsebridge Station, Horsebridge, Kings Somborne, Stockbridge, Hampshire SO20 6PU
Horsebridge Station is a unique and wonderful place to visit for afternoon tea. This beautifully restored Victorian Station has a charming atmosphere, evoked by a bygone age, lovingly preserved in this secluded corner of Hampshire. Teas are served from 2pm - 5pm, May to Sept on selected weekends only, so please check their website before setting out.
www.horsebridgestation.co.uk

The beautifully renovated Victorian Horsebridge Station

The converted mill in Horsebridge

Mottisfont Abbey Garden, House and Estate   (7 Miles)

Mottisfont, near Romsey SO51 0LP

At the heart of this tranquil rural estate is Mottisfont Abbey, set in glorious grounds alongside the fast-flowing River Test. There are many layers of history for the visitor to explore, including the Gothic remains of the original 13th-century Augustinian priory. In the mid 20th century the final private owner, society hostess and patron of the arts Maud Russell, used the Abbey as a base for her racy and intriguing life. The River Test is one of the finest chalk steams in the world and the walled gardens house a National Collection of old-fashioned roses. www.nationaltrust.org.uk/main/w-mottisfont

Danebury Iron Age Hill Fort   (3 miles)

Danebury Down, Stockbridge Road, Stockbridge SO20 6HZ

Danebury Iron Age hill fort is 2500 years old. It is a nationally important Scheduled Ancient Monument and also a Site of Special Scientific Interest...it's also a great place for kite flying!

The site is open all day, every day from April to October (entry is free with ample free parking, and toilets)

www3.hants.gov.uk/countryside/danebury.htm

14. Pitt Down and Farley Mount Country Park

Distance	2.8 miles (4.5km)	Time taken	1 hour
Grade	★★	Postcode	SO21 2JG
Grid Ref	SU419291	Total climb	185 ft (56m)
Map	Ordnance Survey Explorer Map: 1:25000 scale - Sheet 132		
Terrain	Gravel and grass tracks. The tracks are well used and fairly even		
Obstacles	None		
Parking	Pitt Down is situated 3 miles west of Winchester. Head west on Romsey Road, B3404, and then turn right onto Chilbolton Avenue, B3041 and after 0.1 miles turn left onto Sarum Road. After 2 miles, continue straight on at a cross roads, signed Kings Somborne. Continue for 1 mile passing an entrance to Crab Wood and another to West Wood. Follow the road as it bends to the left, then after 0.25 miles and just before the junction, turn right into a parking area. No facilities		

This walk starts at Pitt Down Country Park, which is a beautiful open space of undulating chalk grass land, where families can fly kites, walk dogs and even play cricket (although the ground is rather sloping for serious games). In summer months it's full of wild flowers which attract numerous butterflies, including blue and marble white.

Pitt Down links the car parks to West Wood, where the route follows gravel tracks, passing a number of natural play structures, which are part of a development known as 'It's Okay to Play', borne from a partnership between the Forestry Commission and Winchester City Council, who aim to increase children's enjoyment, activity and involvement in natural environments. This project aims to provide bespoke and exciting natural play facilities at a number of woods in the Winchester district.

The route continues along gravel tracks through mature woodland of mixed conifer and deciduous trees, which is a haven for wildlife. Listen out for the calls of familiar woodland birds, and on early morning walks look out for the many species of deer resident in the woods. The walk passes an entrance to Crab Wood Reserve (an ancient semi natural woodland covering 200 acres to the east of West Wood with Site of Scientific Interest status) then continues to a major crossing of tracks in the middle of West Wood, with an open area of grass and a log seat from which to take in the atmosphere. The final leg follows a wide woodland track leading back to Pitt Down.

A short distance away from Pitt Down is 'The Horse Monument' at Farley Mount, erected in memory of a horse that carried its owner, Paulet St John to a racing victory in 1734, a year after having fallen 25 feet into a chalk pit whilst out fox hunting. The views of the surrounding countryside are worth the short walk to visit the monument which is set in a circular area of grass with two log benches, making it a great place for a picnic.

Walk Description

S. From the parking area go around a green metal barrier, then immediately turn right in front of an information board to follow a grass path down the hill towards West Wood. Keep left alongside a line of trees, passing light blue marker posts to your left.

1. At the bottom of the hill, next to a red marker post, turn right into the forest to walk alongside a wire fence on your left. After 40 yards, go past a green 'West Wood' sign and continue straight on along a gravel track, passing a grass track on your right, and then an earth track on your left. Then, after 525 yards, continue straight on at a crossing of tracks.

2. After another 370 yards, follow the track round to the right and up a short hill. After 330 yards, continue straight on where a path crosses the track and continue up a gentle gradient.

3. As you start to descend, follow the track as it turns right, passing a little used path to your left. Continue as the track gently climbs upward.

4. After 300 yards, continue straight on past a grass track on your right and continue on up the gently rising hill.

5. After 440 yards, as the track sweeps round to the right, continue straight on past a metal barrier on your left (this is an entrance to Crab Wood). Continue along the gravel track through Burrow Copse.

6. After 215 yards, follow the track as it curves to the left, then after another 100 yards, at a point where you can see a metal barrier 250 yards ahead, turn right onto a grass track. Follow this track for 400 yards to a junction of five paths in the centre of Farley Mount Country Park.

7. Take the second path on your left (or the third on your right). Follow this track for 620 yards, passing a carved wooden figure. At a junction with a gravel

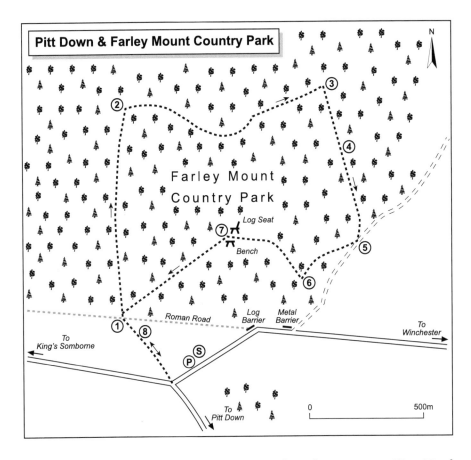

track, turn left passing a large green sign marking the entrance to West Wood
on your right. Continue on into the open park land of Pitt Down Country Park.

8. Bear slightly left as you come into the field, then retrace your steps straight up
the hill, keeping the line of trees on your right, to the parking area at the top
of the hill at the starting point.

The Horse Monument at Farley Mount

To visit the Horse Monument you can walk from Pitt Down but if you prefer to
drive, turn right out of the car park, then after 350 yards, at the junction turn
right. After 320 yards, continue past the first of two parking areas on your right,
and after another 265 yards continue past the second parking area. Then after a
further 670 yards turn left, signed 'Clarendon Way' into the Monument Parking
Area, OS Grid Reference: SU408293. From the parking area, continue along the

Clarendon Way, past a black metal barrier. After 455 yards turn left to follow a footpath up a short slope and through a wooden gate. Continue on up to the monument 125 yards ahead. If you prefer to walk from Pitt Down, it's approximately 1 mile each way. Simply follow the footpaths along the top of Pitt Down, adjacent to the road in the directions above.

Refreshments

The Plough Inn
Main Road, Sparsholt, Nr Winchester SO21 2NW
The Plough started life about 200 years ago as a coach house for Sparsholt Manor, becoming an alehouse just 50 years later. They offer a fine and varied menu, including a children's menu and have a large enclosed garden with picnic tables.
www.theaa.com/pubs/sparsholt-the-plough-inn-376040

The Horse Monument at Farley Mount

Local Attractions

Kids2Day (5.8 miles)
5 Renown Close, Chandlers Ford Industrial Estate, Eastleigh SO53 4HZ
Kids Today is a great indoor children's soft play centre providing two large play structures. The larger area provides three levels for children to explore. The smaller area is secure and great for little ones. They have a tasty menu for kids and provide a comfortable, relaxing environment for parents to enjoy a lovely cup of coffee or tea.
www.kids2day.co.uk/index.html

Sir Harold Hillier Gardens (5.7 miles)
Jermyns Lane, Ampfield, Romsey SO51 0QA
Sir Harold Hillier Gardens (formerly Arboretum) is open all year and offers 180 acres of beauty, inspiration and discovery. Over 42,000 plants from temperate regions around the world grow in a variety of themed landscapes. There are events and exhibitions all year round. Excellent restaurant and summer tea rooms. Family friendly and free entry for children.
www3.hants.gov.uk/hilliergardens

15. Winchester City and Water Meadows

Distance	2.4 miles (3.9km)	Time taken	1 hour 10 mins
Grade	★	Postcode	SO23 9PA
Grid Ref	SU483280	Total climb	45 ft (14m)
Map	Ordnance Survey Explorer Map: 1:25000 scale – Sheet 132		
Terrain	River side footpaths, pavements, back roads and Cathedral grounds		
Obstacles	None		
Parking	Park at Garnier Road Car Park. Garnier Road can be accessed from Junction 10 of the north bound M3, which gets you directly onto the Bar End roundabout; or from Junction 9 south bound by taking the A272 Spitfire Link to Spitfire Roundabout, then take the second exit onto St Catherine's Way, at the next roundabout take the first exit to continue along the A31, and the next roundabout is Bar End roundabout. At Bar End roundabout take the first exit onto Bull Drove, signed to St Cross. Continue onto Garnier Road and past the Park & Ride on your right. Continue under the railway bridge and the parking area is on your left, before crossing the river		

Winchester is a beautiful unspoilt cathedral city on the edge of the South Downs. Being the ancient capital of both Wessex and England, and historical seat of King Alfred the Great, it's packed with historical buildings, monuments and museums, many of which are passed on this walk.

The route starts south of the city beneath St Catherine's Hill to walk along the old Itchen Navigation, which was constructed in 1660 to carry coal and corn to Southampton. The walk follows this water way to join the river Itchen and into pretty gardens in front of an Old Mill House, which is now converted to residential use. Keep a sharp eye out for water voles that live along the river. The route continues up to the City Mill, which is fully restored, powered by the fast flowing River Itchen, and resumed grinding flour in 2004. Further on the walk passes King Alfred's imposing bronze statue and then the Victorian Guildhall before approaching the Cathedral.

The Cathedral was founded in 1079 on the site of an earlier Saxon building and was redesigned in the 14th century. It's worth a visit, especially on Sundays when there's no entrance fee (although a donation is expected), as it includes many interesting features, including the 12th century illuminated Winchester Bible, medieval wall paintings, the tombs of early English kings and those of both Jane Austen and Izaak Walton, and a statue of 'Diver Bill' who saved the Cathedral from sinking into the peat beneath.

From the Cathedral the route continues across the inner close to the half timbered Cheyney Court and on through Kingsgate, with the tiny church of St Swithun-upon-kingsgate above, then past Winchester College. Founded in 1382 by William of Wykeham, Winchester College is the oldest school in England. A little further on you'll pass the Bishops of Winchesters House. Although most of the formerly grand palace is in ruins, the east wing is still home to the Winchester bishops and has spectacular views over the ruins of the 12th century Wolvesey Castle. The route continues along College Walk and through the water meadows alongside the tributary streams of the River Itchen.

Towards the end of the walk the route includes a return trip along the river to the historic, grade I listed St Cross Hospital. Prince Henry de Bliss, Bishop of Winchester, founded St Cross Hospital in the early 12th century to provide refuge and food to needy men. At the hospital you can visit the Norman church, the Brethrens Hall and medieval kitchens. These ancient medieval and Tudor buildings are little changed in form or function, indeed the hospital is still an Almshouse; on request you'll be supplied with the Wayfarer's Dole, a piece of bread and a small beaker of ale.

The English Romantic poet, John Keats, stayed in Winchester during the late summer and early autumn of 1819. He enjoyed a daily walk though the Cathedral Close and water meadows to St Cross. He was so inspired by the natural beauty of Winchester that he wrote his ode *To Autumn* after one of his walks.

Walk Description

S. Exit the Car Park on to Garnier Road. Turn left, then immediately cross the road to find a path signed 'Pilgrims Trail, Winchester 1 mile'. Follow this path with the river on your left along a playing field and then after 440 yards past tennis courts on your right.

1. Continue along the path alongside the river and after 100 yards, turn right up a short path to Domum Road. Turn left onto the road and proceed past Willow Cottage.

2. After 265 yards, at the end of the road, in front of a large white house, bear right onto Wharf Hill. Then, after 100 yards, bear left at a fork towards a small parking area. At the end of the drive, in front of parking spaces, turn left to cross the river directly in front of the Old Mill House.

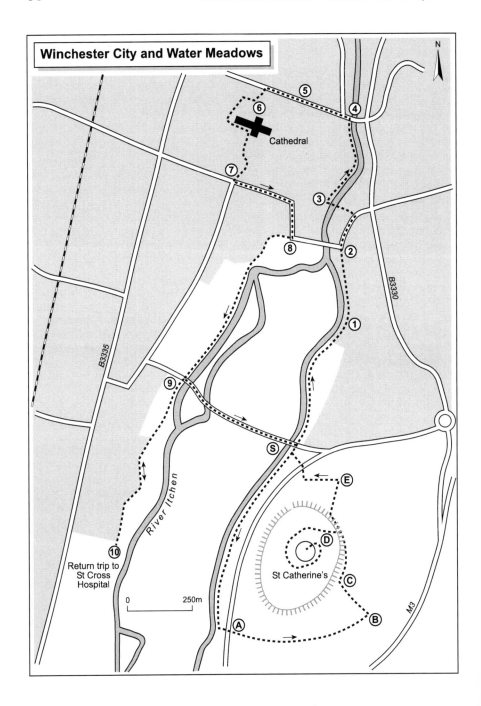

Winchester City and Water Meadows

N

Cathedral

B3330

B3335

River Itchen

Return trip to
St Cross
Hospital

St Catherine's

0   250m

M3

3. Turn right immediately after crossing the first part of the river and follow a footpath with the river on your right. Continue straight on and, after 135 yards, pass a wooden bridge over the river to your right. At this point you might like to stop to feed the ducks and swans. Continue along the river side footpath.

4. After 245 yards, walk up a ramp next to steps onto Bridge Street. If you'd like to visit the City Mill, cross directly over the road. To continue on the walk turn left onto Bridge Street to walk past 'The Bishop on the Bridge' public house. This is a great place to stop for refreshments, especially if the weather allows use of the garden, which looks out over the river. Once refreshed continue along the High Street towards the statue of King Alfred and straight on along The Broadway.

5. Continue past Abbey House and the Information Centre, both on your left and straight on past Colebrook Street. Continue along The Broadway past Debenhams on your left, then immediately turn left under the building supported by stone pillars. Follow the pavement to cross Market Lane and continue towards the Cathedral.

6. Turn right in front of black railings and walk alongside these to the front of the Cathedral. Continue around the Cathedral and under the stone arches,

The Bishops House has spectacular views over the ruins of the 12th century Wolvesey Castle

Winchester Cathedral grounds are commonly used for a lunch time picnic

then bear right to cross the Inner Close. Continue past the Education Centre bearing left onto Dome Alley, and then follow a footpath signed for 'College, Wolvesey Castle & Water Meadows' to leave the Inner Close through St Swithun's Gate, adjacent to the timber framed Cheyney Court.

7. Once through the gates, turn left under the arches of 'The church of St Swithon Upon Kingsgate' onto Kingsgate Street. After 15 yards, turn left onto College Street and continue past Winchester College to the end of the road after 300 yards. At the junction with Collage Walk you can access Wolvesey Castle through the black gates to your left. Leaving Wolvesely Castle gates behind you, continue onto College Walk (or from College Street turn right onto College Walk).

8. After 100 yards, at a junction turn right and after a further 85 yards, at the end of the road, turn left through black railings onto a path along the River Itchen. Continue along the river side footpath, with Winchester College playing fields across the river to your right.

9. After 0.5 miles go through a gap in the fence line to the right of a wooden gate, then at Garnier Road cross over bearing slightly right to cross the river in front of a flint building, to follow 'The Clarendon Way' alongside the river, signed to St Cross Hospital. After 125 yards, continue straight on along the surfaced footpath as the river turns away to the left. From this point on you'll glimpse views of St Catherine's Hill through the trees to your left.

   After another 100 yards, you'll pass a triangular picnic table on your left, providing a good spot for a rest stop. Continue straight on along the footpath, then after 135 yards turn right off the Clarendon Way to cross a small wooden footbridge. Continue onto a tarmac residential road, then after 90 yards, at a cross roads next to a timber frame cottage (The Old Farmhouse), turn left onto St Cross Back Street. There are many very old houses along this ancient road.

10. After 225 yards, continue straight on past a white barrier to cross the road and continue under a stone archway to enter 'The Hospital of St Cross and Almshouse of Noble Poverty'. The porters lodge is on the left under the archway of the square tower ahead.

   From St Cross Hospital retrace your steps to go back around the white barrier opposite the main entrance to the hospital, and then continue straight on along St Cross Back Street. After 225 yards, at the cross roads, turn right next to 'The Old Farmhouse', and after 90 yards continue straight on to cross the wooden footbridge. Then turn left onto The Clarendon Way to walk alongside a stream.

   After 375 yards, turn right onto Garnier Road, then immediately cross over, in front of double wooden gates, to use the pavement and continue along the road. After 35 yards continue straight on past 'The Pump House' (now business premises for 'remarkable') on your right. Then, after another 100 yards, cross the river over a wooden footbridge, and continue along Garnier Road.

After 215 yards, cross over to use the pavement, and after another 175 yards cross the Itchen Navigation and then turn right into the parking area at the starting point.

St Catherine's Hill Romp

Distance	1.8 miles (2.8km)	Time taken	1 hour
Grade	★ ★ ★ ★ ★		
Terrain	Surfaced riverside footpath, grass and leaf litter footpaths, small but numerous steps on the descent		
Obstacles	A series of 106 small steps		

If you fancy a romp up St Catherine's Hill it is possible to do this with an all-terrain pushchair as long as you're feeling fit, are well used to pushing up steep hills and don't mind the 106 steps on the decent. This route starts from the same parking area as the walk above and follows the river in the opposite direction, then up the pretty 'Plague Pit Valley' to access the rear of the mount which has a relatively short, but steep push directly up the hill. This route avoids pushing along paths which cross the steep slopes on an angle, but please be extremely careful to keep a firm grip on your pushchair on all hilly sections. Towards the end of the route down, after negotiating the steps, there's a short chalk slope which can become slippery, so needs to be negotiated with additional care. It's recommended that you use a leash to strap the pushchair to your wrist on any hilly sections.

With all the caution given, this is a wonderful walk and well worth the views over Winchester, St Cross Hospital and the Itchen Valley. St Catherine's Hill is a Site of Scientific Interest and a worthy part of the East Hampshire's Area of Outstanding Beauty. The hill is a 143 acre, flower rich chalk grassland attracting an abundance of butterflies. The hill has been used by people for 3000 years, well before the foundation of Winchester. The summit has deep Iron Age ramparts constructed in the 3rd century BC, which are a scheduled ancient monument. In the middle of the summit, under the cover of a copse of beech trees, is a ruined 12th century Norman Chapel and nearby is a mysterious Mizmaze, chiselled out of the chalk in the 17th century, and comprising nine nested squares and measuring over 600 yards long.

Walk Description

S. Leave the parking area heading away from the road, with the river on your right, to go between black bollards and walk along a surfaced riverside footpath. Glimpse views of St Cross Hospital through the trees to your right as you walk alongside the river, which is full of wildlife, most notably moorhens, coots, ducks, swans.

A. After 825 yards, turn left to go through a well signed small wooden gate into St Catherine's Hill Reserve, which is managed by Hampshire and Isle of Wight Wildlife Trust. Cross the enclosure and go through another small wooden gate. Continue straight on, passing a ladder of steps to your left, to cross a short section of uneven ground to find a smooth grass footpath after 35 yards. Follow this path up a gentle rise along the valley bottom, curving to the left around the foot of St Catherine's Hill.

B. After 630 yards, at a junction of grass paths, 150 yards before a stock handling pen, turn left onto a reasonably well used path heading to the summit of St Catherine's hill. After 25 yards, keep right at a fork to continue directly up a steep hill, passing hawthorn bushes on your left (avoid using the paths which cross the slope with a pushchair due to the risk of tipping over). After another 45 yards continue up the hill under trees, again steep and with a couple of small roots to negotiate.

C. After 75 yards, follow the path round to the right into trees to walk along a wide ditch forming part of the deep ramparts of this Iron Age fort. After another 220 yards, at a raised crossing of paths, turn left towards the summit and a 'St Catherine's Hill Mizmaze' information board. The Mizmaze is thought to have existed since the late 17th century, but its use is not known. From this point you can explore the summit, look out for the ruined Norman Chapel hidden amongst the beech trees ahead and take in the views.

D. Return to the Mizmaze information board and follow the footpath back to the ramparts, then turn left to continue along the footpath along the rampart ditch. After 90 yards, turn right to make your way down the hill with a wooden rail to your left. After 50 yards, continue down a long series of steps. After 46 steps you'll pass a bench and, after another 60 steps, follow the path round to the left along a flat section and a rest from steps.

E. After 150 yards, follow the path as it turns to the right and continue down a slope. This slope is often slippery so take great care with a firm grip on your pushchair. Go through a small wooden gate at the bottom of the slope. Continue for 25 yards to go through another gate, and then walk under a red brick arch to return to the parking area at the start.

Refreshments

The Bishop on the Bridge
1 High Street, Winchester SO23 9JX
This lovely traditional pub stands elegantly on the banks of the River Itchen and offers stunning views from its garden terrace. It's a great place to enjoy a meal or a coffee.
www.fullers.co.uk/rte.asp?id=243&itemid=24&task=View

Local Attractions

INTECH Science Centre (7.5 miles)
Telegraph Way, Morn Hill, Winchester SO21 1HZ
This is a hands-on interactive science and technology centre and the UK's largest capacity digital Planetarium! Featuring 100 interactive exhibits, which demonstrate the science and technology of the world around us in an engaging and exciting way. The Astrium Planetarium is a digital state-of-the-art theatre with a variety of shows to suit all interests.
www.intech-uk.com

Marwell Wildlife Park (10 miles)
Thompsons Lane, Colden Common, Winchester SO21 1JH
A visit to Marwell Wildlife is a chance to get close to the wonders of the natural world – and play a part in helping to save them. The 140 acre park is home to over 250 exotic and endangered species, in beautiful, landscaped surroundings. Enjoy spectacular views of the African Valley, while you eat and drink at Café Graze, or its attached picnic area. There's also a free road train to help you get around, and three play areas where children can run wild.
www.marwell.org.uk

The Great Hall and Round Table
Southgate Street, Winchester SO23 8GJ
The Great Hall is the first and finest of all 13th century halls, with the greatest symbol of medieval mythology, The Round Table of King Arthur. Winchester Castle dates from the reign of William the Conqueror (1066-1087). Although now known to have been constructed in the late 13th Century, and painted in its present form for King Henry VIII, the table has for centuries been venerated by generations of tourists as the mysterious table of King Arthur.
www3.hants.gov.uk/greathall.ht

16. Alresford Town and River Walk

Distance	2.6 miles (4.3km)	Time taken	1 hour 15 mins
Grade	★★	Postcode	SO24 9JQ
Grid Ref	SU588324	Total climb	110 ft (34m)
Map	Ordnance Survey Explorer Map: 1:25000 scale – Sheet 132		
Terrain	Pavements, riverside surfaced footpaths and a short section of footpath along the edge of an arable field (which can get overgrown in summer months)		
Obstacles	None		
Parking	Turn off the A31 between Winchester and Alton onto the B3047 into Alresford, then follow signs for the station. The station car park is Pay & Display, so don't forget to buy a ticket. If you are not intending to go on the stream trains then there's a good number of free parking spaces, limited to 2 hours (except Sundays and Bank Holidays), along Broad Street. There are public toilets opposite the police station on Station Road		

New Alresford, originally known as New Market, is a pretty market town known for its traditional and specialist shops and old fashioned inns. The town originated 800 years ago in the early 13th century as a place for rural trade, and Broad Street at the towns centre was made sufficiently wide to accommodate sheep fairs and other rural commerce. At around the same time a very large lake was formed to provide power for the mills and fish for Winchester Bishop, Godfrey de Lucy, who lived in a grand palace at Bishop's Sutton. A remnant of the lake survives today as Old Alresford Pond, situated at the bottom of Broad Street behind The Globe Inn (which has lovely lakeside gardens).

Great fires in the 17th century destroyed many of the houses along Broad Street, which were rebuilt in the elegant Georgina red brick seen today. The Old Fire Station, seen at the bottom of Broad Street, was erected by the Bailiff and Burgesses of New Alresford in 1881.

This walk starts at the railway station, home to the Watercress Steam Trains. The railway came to Alresford in 19th century to distribute local produce, including watercress, to a wider market. A ten mile stretch between Alresford and Alton is preserved today attracting visitors wishing to relive nostalgic times. The first part of this walk follows the Millennium Trail which has a series of boards providing information about the area.

The route passes St John the Baptist Church, down Broad Street and past the many interesting and historic buildings, including the early 18th century Arle House. It then continues along the tranquil River Arle, home to a wealth of wildlife,

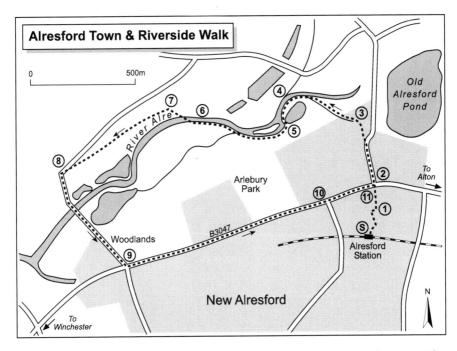

including water voles, kingfishers, herons, otters, brown trout and egrets. The riverside footpath passes the picturesque old Fulling Mill, a timber frame thatched building which straddles the river. Here spun wool was scoured and pounded with mallets to create a fine weave. There are many ducks along this section so don't forget to take plenty of bread for them.

The route continues on past the end of 'The Dean' and into an increasingly rural landscape, where the river is overhung by large trees. It then crosses the river at the quaint 'Eel House', built in the 1820s, with three brick channels designed to accommodate eel traps as the water rushes underneath. The final leg of the route takes you along Winchester Road, passing an old hexagonal toll house, 'Turnpike House', and then continues along 'The Avenue', which is shaded by two lines of large limes. In spring this section is lined with daffodils.

Walk description

S. Leave the station car park through the main entrance onto station Road. You'll see an information board to your right as you leave the car park.

1. After 50 yards, immediately after the police station, turn right into a churchyard. Walk around a metal barrier, and then turn left to walk through the church yard and past the church itself on your right.

Continue along the path bearing left around a white house and down to West Street, alongside Barclays Bank on your right. Turn left onto West Street and, after 55 yards, continue straight on past the top of Station Road. Then after another 25 yards, at a pedestrian crossing, cross over the road and turn right to make your way back up to Broad Street.

2. Turn left down Broad Street, signed Basingstoke and Old Alresford, and continue to the bottom of the hill. After 235 yards, next to Pineapple House Antiques (and opposite the Old Fire Station), bear left to walk down Mill Hill.

3. After 75 yards, opposite an information board on your right, turn left onto Ladywell Lane. Continue along this lane (there is often a slight overflow of water from the natural springs running across the lane as it bends to the right). After another 140 yards, bear right in front of Arle House to follow a footpath to The River Arle. Towards the end of this footpath, on your left, is a Memorial Garden (with a red brick porch entrance), presented to the community by the late Sir Francis Lindley. Continue along the footpath to walk alongside the river for 200 yards.

4. Along the way you'll pass the picturesque old Fulling Mill, a timber frame thatched building which straddles the river. This section of the river is teeming

The picturesque old Fulling Mill straddles the tranquil River Arle in Alresford

with wildlife, most obviously swans, ducks (don't forget bread for them) and trout.

5. At the end of the path, turn right to cross the end of a road, 'The Dean', and continue along the riverside footpath. After 150 yards, continue straight on past a kissing gate on your left (entrance to a recreational ground with a play ground) and continue along the riverside footpath.

6. After 380 yards you'll come to 'Eel House' where the footpath crosses the River Arle as it goes around the building. Continue along the opposite bank and, after another 50 yards, cross a small brick footbridge to continue along the riverside footpath.

7. Follow the footpath up a short slope, then past a stile on your right. After a few yards walk across the top of a driveway and continue along the footpath, to the left of a private parking area, with a post and rail fence on your right. As you follow the footpath through trees there's a short section which can get a little overgrown in summer months (keep little hands in to avoid any nettles). The footpath then runs along the left hand edge of an arable field for 300 yards (it's a little awkward as the ground slopes across the path).

8. At the end of the path continue straight on to join Drove Lane. After 75 yards, follow the road as it turns left, passing Wayfarers Walk on your right. Take care along this section and walk on the outside of the bend to improve your visibility to oncoming traffic. After 200 yards the road crosses the river, then after another 300 yards push up a short hill to reach Winchester Road.

9. Turn left to walk along the pavement back towards Alresford centre. After 200 yards you'll pass the old toll house, the pavement then starts to drop away from the road and continues under an avenue of large lime trees. After 620 yards you'll pass Arlebury Park Recreation Ground.

10. At the end of the footpath continue straight on to walk down Pound Hill (a short residential street running parallel to Winchester Road). Then, at the bottom of a little hill, continue straight on across the top of The Dean and on up West Street. After 100 yards, continue past Alresford Gallery and, after another 55 yards, cross the road at the pedestrian crossing used earlier, then turn left to continue along West Street towards the town centre.

11. After 25 yards cross the top of Station Road, then after another 55 yards turn right just before Barclays Bank. Bear right next to the white house in front of the church and follow the footpath through the church yard. Turn right where the path forks, then turn left onto Station Road and continue back to the car park at the starting point.

Refreshments

Tiffins Tea Room
West Street, Alresford SO24 9AR
At Tiffins Tea Room you can enjoy a relaxed atmosphere either inside or outside in a secluded courtyard. They serve coffees, teas, hot chocolate, light lunches, a variety of snacks and homemade cakes.
www.caracoli.co.uk

The Globe on the Lake
20 The Soke, Alresford SO24 9DB
The Globe is a 17th century coaching inn, pub and restaurant, situated by the lake with a gorgeous lakeside garden. The Globe offers freshly prepared food, using local produce.
www.alresford.org/pubs.php

Local attractions

The Mid Hants Railway 'Watercress Line'
The Railway Station, Alresford SO24 9JG
Sit back, relax, and watch mile after mile of beautiful Hampshire countryside pass you by. The soothing sounds of the steam engine with the beat of the exhaust can be heard over the clickety clack of the wheels passing over the rails.
www.watercressline.co.uk

A steam train on the Watercress line in Alresford

Hinton Ampner
Bramdean, near AlresfordSO24 0LA
The vision of one man, Hinton Ampner, is best known for its magnificent garden with stunning views to the south. The elegant country house was remodelled by Ralph Dutton, the 8th, and last, Lord Sherborne, in 1960 after a devastating fire. The house contains his collection of Georgian and Regency furniture, Italian pictures and objects d'art. The gardens were also laid out by Ralph Dutton and are widely acknowledged as a masterpiece of 20th century design, mixing formal and informal planting, providing all year round interest
www.nationaltrust.org.uk/main/w-hintonampnergarden

17. Micheldever Wood

Distance	1.8 miles (2.9km)	Time taken	1 hour 15 mins
Grade	★	Postcode	SO21 1PP
Grid Ref	SU530362	Total climb	135 ft (41m)
Map	Ordnance Survey Explorer Map: 1:25000 scale - Sheet 132		
Terrain	Gravel tracks, woodland paths and tracks		
Obstacles	None		
Parking	There's a large parking area off Northington Lane which is accessed from the A33, nearly 2 miles South of Micheldever. Turn onto Northington Road from a section of duel carriageway. Pass under the M3 and continue through the woods for just less than a mile, then turn left into the car park amongst the trees		

Micheldever Wood is famous for a spectacular display of bluebells that carpet the woodland floor during spring and early summer months. This large ancient woodland is approximately 536 acres of mixed deciduous, predominantly beech, with some oak and conifer interspersed. The wood supports an abundance of wildlife including roe deer, fallow deer, many species of woodland birds and numerous wild flowers attracting a myriad of butterflies.

In addition there are several sites of archaeological interest, including several Iron and Bronze Age earthworks. Indeed, there's an archaeological trail around the wood taking you to each site of interest, in most cases with an information board to explain details of each site.

The walk described here starts along sweeping gravel tracks passing an Iron Age banjo enclosure and an early Bronze Age burial mount. It then follows a grass track through a widened avenue of trees, planted in 1992 to commemorate the 40th anniversary of the Queens accession to the throne. The species chosen - such as aspen, oak, holly, wild rose and thirty six more - are all native to Britain and indigenous to the region.

As the route continues into thicker trees, the woodland floor becomes devoid of undergrowth, and there's a slight detour to visit the Early Bronze Age Barrows. The route continues along woodland tracks under a dense covering of trees to emerge onto a gravel track.

The final leg of the route continues along wide gravel tracks, and towards the end passes a children's natural play structure. The natural play structure is part of a development known as 'It's Okay to Play', borne from a partnership between the Forestry Commission and Winchester City Council who aim to increase children's enjoyment, activity and involvement in natural environments. This project aims to provide bespoke and exciting natural play facilities at a number of woods in the Winchester district.

Walk Description

S. Start at the 'Micheldever Wood Archaeological Trail' information board, opposite the car park entrance. Continue away from the car park to turn right onto a gravel track. After 185 yards, follow the track as it turns to the left and on up a gentle hill.

1. After 350 yards, you'll come to an 'Iron Age Banjo Enclosure' information board and site. Once you're ready to move on, continue along the gravel track.

2. After another 245 yards, at a junction, you can detour left, as indicated by a green footprint post, to visit the second archaeological site, an 'Early Bronze Age Burial Mound'. You can see the information board 85 yards ahead. Once you've satisfied your interest, retrace your steps back to the gravel track and turn left to continue along the route. If you don't fancy the detour just carry straight on past this junction. After 230 yards continue straight on at a crossing of tracks.

3. Then, after a further 245 yards, at a crossing of tracks, turn left to follow a grass track. The first short section of this track can become a little bumpy if the forestry vehicles have been active in wet weather but it soon clears. As you continue down a slope you'll see a row of labelled trees and shrubs on each side of the widened track. They were planted to commemorate the 40th anniversary of the Queens accession to the throne. After 400 yards, at the end of the planted area, before continuing up the hill, you'll pass an information board detailing the species planted. Continue straight on, passing a turning on your left after 85 yards.

4. After a further 45 yards, at a junction, turn right to see 'Early Bronze Age Barrows' together with a relevant information board. After inspecting the site, retrace your

Early Bronze Age Barrows in Micheldever Woods

steps to walk past the top of the junction, heading directly away from the information board. Continue along this woodland track under the cover of trees.

5. After 230 yards, at a crossing of tracks, with a small pit 25 yards to your right, turn left. Then, after 65 yards, at a junction forming a small grass triangle, turn right. After 90 yards, pass another pit on your right and continue over a small undulation in the path. After 85 yards, pass a turning on your left.

6. Then, after a further 50 yards, continue straight to cross a track and follow a wider gravel track. After 480 yards, you can detour left onto a small footpath and in 35 yards you'll find an 'It's Okay to Play' natural play facility. Once you've climbed through the tunnel and slid down the pole, retrace your steps and turn left onto the gravel track. If you don't fancy the detour just carry

straight on past this junction. Continue for a further 100 yards, and with a metal barrier ahead, turn left. After 60 yards, turn right into the parking area at the start of the walk.

Refreshments

The Half Moon and Spread Eagle (2.7 miles)
Winchester Road, Micheldever SO21 3DG
This is a traditional village pub, in the picturesque Dever valley, with a friendly atmosphere and good pub food. Good sized garden with plenty of picnic tables. www.hmse.co.uk

Local Attractions

The Grange (2.2 miles)
Northington SO24 9TG
The Grange was one of the earliest houses in England built in classical Geek Revival style. The original design was later altered to resemble a Greek temple. Visitors can walk about the lawns overlooking a lake and view the exterior of the building, but cannot currently view the inside. The Grange can be reached by car following English Heritage signs just south of Swarraton. Alternatively you can walk half a mile from Northington Church (SO24 9TH, OS Grid Reference: SU810420). www.english-heritage.org.uk/daysout/properties/northington-grange

The Grange, a classical Geek Revival style house in a lake land setting

18. Woodmancott Farm Tracks and Woodland Walk

Distance	3.5 miles (5.6km)	Time taken	1 hour 15 mins
Grade	★★★	Postcode	SO21 3BL
Grid Ref	SU562425	Total climb	190 ft (58m)
Map	Ordnance Survey Explorer Map: 1:25000 scale – Sheet 144		
Terrain	Gravel tracks, woodland tracks and paths. There is one short section of footpath which is a bit narrow through low undergrowth, making it a little awkward for pushchairs		
Obstacles	None		
Parking	Woodmancott is just east of the M3, between Winchester and Basingstoke. From junction 7 of the M3, take the A30 in a south westerly direction. After nearly 2 miles continue onto the A33, then after 2.3 miles turn left and continue over the M3. After 1 mile, as the road bends to the right, go straight on into Woodmancott. Continue past some houses on your left then turn left to park on the track between trees alongside St James Church, Woodmancott		

Woodmancott is a tiny hamlet consisting of a church and a few farm houses in the parish of Micheldever. In the Domesday Survey of 1086 Woodmancott Manor was held by the New Minster at Winchester. It continued in the possession of Hyde Abbey until the Dissolution, when it became crown property. In 1544 Henry VIII granted the manor to Winchester College, where it was held until 1974.

This walk starts in Woodmancott adjacent to the formerly medieval Church of St James, which was burnt down on Easter Day in 1854 and rebuilt from flint with stone dressings, in a Norman style, in the following year. Traces of early civilization at Woodmancott include a Neolithic flint arrowhead and two Bronze Age barrows. The route follows gravel farm tracks through College Wood, where Roman remains such as tiles and pottery have been found. It then proceeds towards Popham, with views over the surrounding countryside, much of which is still owned by Winchester College.

The route continues through Popham, a small collection of houses with a lovely village pond in a tranquil setting, then passes Popham Court which is close to the site of a medieval village (which has been mostly erased by the construction of roads). The walk continues through Popham Down Copse, which is the highest point in the parish of Woodmancott, and a haven for wildlife. Woodmancott estate is used for shooting so the woodland is interspersed with open areas of sweeping grass land and crops, such as artichoke, kale and maize, which provide cover for game birds. As you follow footpaths through the woods you may see peacocks foraging across the open fields in, perhaps an unusually natural environment for this ornate bird.

The final leg of the route follows another gravel farm track past conifer plantations in various stages of maturity and back past Woodmancott House to St James Church at the starting point.

Walk Description

S. Walk along the track away from the road, with St James Church on your right, alongside a lovely avenue of trees to your right and on a slight incline towards College Wood ahead.

1. After 300 yards, pass a track to your right, then after another 120 yards continue straight on over a crossing of tracks at the top of the hill. Follow the gravel track as it sweeps to the right and opens out for great views to Popham Down Copse ahead and open fields to your left.

2. Immediately after passing a hedge line on your left, turn left onto a gravel track alongside the hedge on your left. Follow the track down a hill, and up quite steeply on the other side of the dip.

3. At the top of the hill, turn left onto a similar track, this time with a hedge to your right. Continue along the track as it turns slightly right, towards the houses ahead.

4. After 320 yards, once you've past the first house, immediately turn right to follow a tarmac road along the front of the row of houses. Continue along the road to pass a duck pond on your left. There's a bench here – perhaps a place to stop and feed the ducks.

5. At a junction, just after the pond, turn right to follow a road past houses and a large converted barn, 'Popham Court Farm', and continue onto a gravel track.

6. After 475 yards, continue straight on as you pass a barn with green barriers across its entrance to your left, and a track to your right. Continue as the gravel track turns to a grass track which, after 600 yards, takes you on into 'Popham Down Copse'. Follow the track through the woods.

7. After 300 yards, at a crossing of paths, turn right in front of a footpath finger-post, to follow a track. After 10 yards, turn right onto a footpath. There are a couple yellow footpath badges on the trees to indicate the route. Continue to

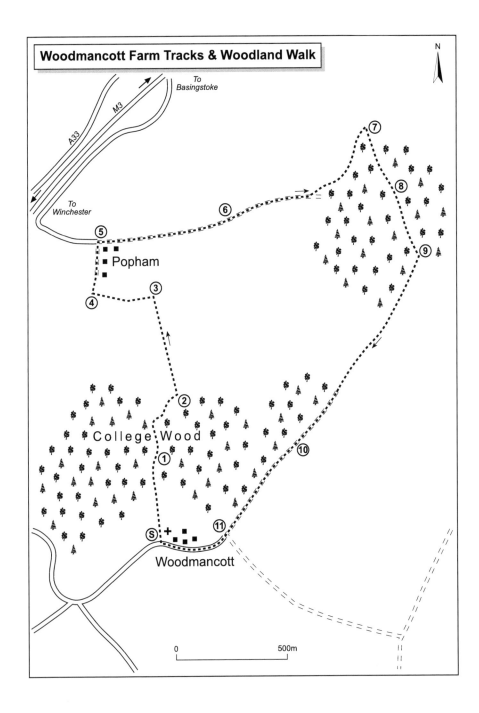

follow the footpath across a clearing with young trees. This short section across the clearing is a bit narrow through low undergrowth, making it a little awkward for pushchairs.

8. At a junction, continue straight on over a track to follow the footpath through the trees and then up onto a second track. At this junction turn right onto the track then, almost immediately turn left to continue along the footpath as it crosses the top of an arable field. There are often a number of peacocks in the field to your right, so keep an eye out for them.

   Continue around the corner of the arable field, then after 50 yards turn left to follow the footpath back into the woods. Continue through the trees and bare right as you approach a fenced clearing of planted conifers.

9. Follow the footpath to cross over a gravel track, to cut the corner and, after 25 yards, turn right onto the same track (after it's turned through ninety degrees), which is signed 'Bridleway' and heads towards a large conifer plantation. Follow the bridleway with the conifer plantation on the left.

10. After 700 yards, pass a turning to your right, then after another 300 yards continue straight on at the end of the plantation, with a woodland on your right.

An avenue of trees leading up to College Wood at Woodmancott

11. After another 600 yards, continue past a turning on the left and Woodmancott House on your right. Follow the road as it bends to the right, past a row of farm houses and then buildings. Then as you pass a turning to your left, turn right off the road onto a gravel footpath, to walk in front of a red telephone box. Continue past St James Church and to the starting point.

Refreshments

The Northbrook Arms (2.4 miles)
East Stratton, Winchester SO21 3DU
Situated in the picturesque village of East Stratton, this pub is owned by Lord Northbrook and has been in the family many generations. Interesting culinary fare using quality local produce. Garden and picnic tables are across the road in front of the pub.
www.thenorthbrookarms.com

Local Attractions

Airbourne Aviation
Popham Airfield, Coxford Down, Micheldever SO21 3BD
Treat yourselves to the most exhilarating experience of your life...A flight in a fast, modern ultralight plane or autogyro! Or try a simulator training session. The facilities at Popham are fantastic and the airfield is set in a beautiful location.
www.flymac.co.uk

Sheep pastures near College Wood

19. Selborne Common

Distance	2.3 miles (3.7km)	Time taken	1 hour 15 mins
Grade	★ ★ ★ ★	Postcode	GU34 3JR
Grid Ref	SU742335	Total climb	310 ft (95m)
Map	Ordnance Survey Explorer Map: 1:25000 scale – Sheet 133		
Terrain	Woodland footpaths, including a steep climb and a zig-zag descent		
Obstacles	There are no obstacles per se, however the walk finishes down zig-zag steps. The path itself isn't steep due to the zig-zag route taken, however at each turn there are 4 or 5 small wooden steps to negotiate, (this is not a problem if your pushchair is tipped back onto its rear wheels and carefully lowered down each step). A pushchair leash is recommended for this section and it's advisable to have a look at these steps from the bottom (at point 1), before venturing up the Bostal path, so that you can satisfy yourself that your little one will enjoy the final bumpy descent		
Parking	Selborne is situated 4 miles South East of Alton. From the A31, head South on the A339 and continue onto the B3006, Selborne Road. As you come into Selborne, continue past the church and post office, then turn right immediately after the Selborne Arms to park in the village car park		

Selborne is a beautiful rural village famous for its association with the 18th Century naturalist Gilbert White, who was born in the village in 1720. In pursuit of his study of the local flora and fauna, in 1753 and 1779 Gilbert White, and his brother John, constructed the Zig-Zag and Bostal Paths up Selborne Hanger to the common above. Selborne Hill and Common are little changed since the days of Gilbert White and are great examples of ancient woodland pasture and steep beech hanger, so characteristic of this part of Hampshire and now preserved by the National Trust.

This fragment of ancient landscape lies within the East Hampshire Area of Outstanding Natural Beauty and is of great ecological importance, being a designated Site of Special Scientific Interest and a Special Area of Conservation. The hanger supports a distinct array of flowers and the woods above are home to many rare invertebrates, including the ash-black slug, five species of Ctenophora cranefly and countless butterflies.

The walk starts with a climb along the Bostal Path up Selborne Hanger. It's a fairly steep but very pleasant woodland footpath. At the top is a superb view of the historic

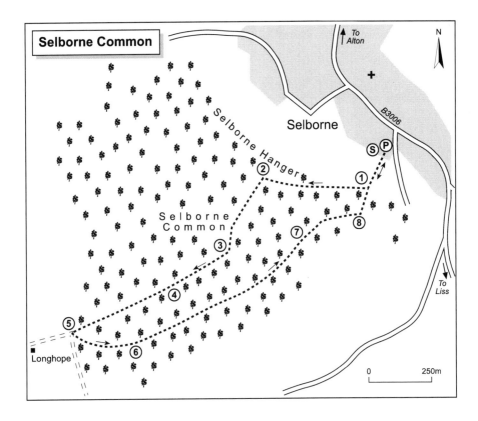

Church of St Mary's and the Lythes beyond. The route continues with an elongated loop around Selborne Common, described by Gilbert White as 'a vast hill of chalk'. The ancient common offers a tranquil haven some 300 feet above the village. The route finishes down the infamous Zig-Zag Path, at the top of which is White's Wishing Stone and splendid views over the village and the surrounding countryside.

Walk description

S. Start near the entrance to the car park, level with the back garden of the Selborne Arms, to follow a pretty footpath signed 'Footpath to Selborne Common' heading away from the road.

1. After 250 yards, go through a wooden gate. This gate swings widely open and is difficult to handle one handed so make sure your pushchair is securely parked before attempting to unlatch the gate. Once through the gate, turn right in front of an information board, then immediately bear left to follow The

Bostal Path which climbs diagonally up Selborne Hanger. It's a fairly steep climb but there's a bench two thirds of the way up so that you can catch your breath before continuing to the top. Once at the top there's another metal bench which has a wonderful view over Selborne Church and the Lythes below.

2. From the bench, bear left to push directly up the slope past a solitary beech tree and to cross another path. Continue directly away from the view of the church along a footpath for 85 yards, to a wooden kissing gate. Go through the gate to enter 'Sheep Down'. Then follow a footpath and, after 50 yards, you'll reach a clearing with the ground dropping away to your right. Turn left along a woodland track and up a gentle slope, which is a little uneven in places.

3. After 175 yards, at a junction, turn right onto a level grass track. Then, after 350 yards, you'll come to a large open area of grass, gorse and bracken to your right (don't be confused by previous smaller open areas, this one is the size of a football pitch).

4. Continue along the path with the open area to your right and, after 85 yards, where the path forks, turn left into the woods. Continue along this wide woodland path, enjoying the diversity of flora and fauna, including in summer months woodland flowers and countless butterflies.

5. After 350 yards, with a wooden gate ahead, turn left in front of a finger post, then continue down a gentle slope and, after 20 yards, turn left again in front of another finger post, signed 'Footpath to Selborne'

6. After 220 yards, bear left at a fork in the footpath and continue through a very pretty mixed deciduous woodland, in summer months densely donned with foxgloves and other summer flowers.

7. After a little more than 0.5 miles, in front of a beech tree, bear left at a minor fork onto the more used path. Then after another 50 yards, at a junction, turn right to go through a wooden kissing gate and follow a footpath down the slope.

8. After 75 yards, at a fork in the path, bear right along the wider path, alongside a hedge. After another 35 yards you'll come to a metal bench to your left, from where there are far reaching views over Selborne. In front of the bench is Gilbert Whites 'Wishing Stone' at the top of the famous zig-zag path. Once you've made your wishes continue down a footpath to the left of the wishing stone. This path, as the name suggests, zig-zags down the steep hill punctuated with clusters of small steps on each turn (obstacle).

After the last zig or zag, at the bottom of the hill, with the information board on your left, turn right to go through the wooden gate. Then follow the footpath back to the car park at the starting point.

Refreshments

The Selborne Arms
High Street, Selborne GU34 3JR
A traditional village pub with real fires, a friendly atmosphere and a large garden with children's play area. The menu offers a range of traditional and innovative dishes which showcase local and homemade produce. They also have a lunchtime snack menu and a wide range of soft drinks for the children.
www.selbornearms.co.uk/index.htm

Tea Parlour at Gilbert White's House
High Street (opposite the church), Selborne GU34 3JH
Delicious refreshments are served in the elegantly restored dining room. They offer a selection of speciality teas, homemade cakes and light lunches. They've been awarded a Tea Council Award of Excellence for 2010, one of only two Hampshire establishments to receive this highly sought-after guarantee of quality.
www.gilbertwhiteshouse.org.uk/opening-times/tea-parlour

Local attractions

Gilbert White's House and The Oates Museum
High Street (opposite the church), Selborne GU34 3JH
Home of the 18th Century naturalist, Gilbert White, this historic house standing in more than 20 acres of formal gardens, houses furnished rooms, original manuscript and the exhibitions of Frank Oates, the Victorian explorer and Captain Laurence Oates, hero of Scott's ill-fated expedition to the South Pole.
www.gilbertwhiteshouse.org.uk

A fallen tree on Selborne Common

20. Selborne Lythes

Distance	2.9 miles (4.7km)	Time taken	1 hour 15 mins
Grade	★ ★ ★	Postcode	GU34 3JR
Grid Ref	SU742335	Total climb	205 ft (63m)
Map	Ordnance Survey Explorer Map: 1:25000 scale – Sheet 133		
Terrain	Village roads, grass and woodland footpaths, farm tracks. A short section of farm track, on the last leg in Coombe Wood, gets deeply rutted on both sides. This was suitable for pushchairs during fair weather but is likely to get very muddy in winter months		
Obstacles	There are three obstacles on this walk where two people are recommended in order to lift your pushchair: 1. To exit the church yard into the meadow below you need to go through a narrow kissing gate. The space is too narrow for pushchairs but the gate is light weight and can easily be lifted off its hinges, which has evidently been done frequently 2. At the bottom of the church meadow, in order to reach the first Lythe you need to cross a wooden foot bridge. At the start of this bridge there's a barrier across half the width at approximately 2'6" high. With two people it's easy enough to lift your pushchair over this barrier 3. Towards the end of the walk, in order to get onto Huckers Lane, which leads up to The Queens Inn, you need to cross three consecutive railway sleepers placed on the ground approximately 1 metre apart. They're only 6" high, designed for horses to be able to walk over but to prevent motor bikes from passing. Again this barrier is easily negotiated with two people		
Parking	Selborne is situated 4 miles South East of Alton. From the A31, head South on the A339 and continue onto the B3006, Selborne Road. As you come into Selborne, continue past the church and post office, and then turn right immediately after the Selborne Arms to park in the village car park		

This walk starts below Selborne Hanger and begins by passing though the picturesque village of Selborne. The route takes you across the Plestor (once a place for fairs and markets), and on past the historic church of St Mary's. On the site of a Saxon church, St Mary's contains two magnificent stained glass windows commemorating Gilbert White, the local 18th Century literary naturalist, whose

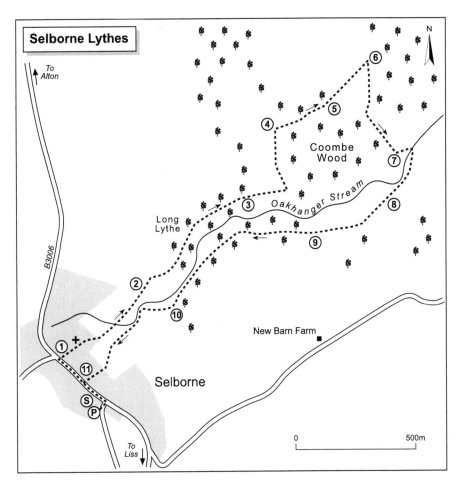

grave can be found to the north of the church. Published in 1789, his book *The Natural History and Antiquities of Selborne* was based on 40 years of observations of the flora and fauna around the village, including several discoveries, such as the harvest mouse. Indeed he was the first to report the importance of earthworms in improving soil. Also in the church yard is the trunk of an ancient yew tree, with a 26 foot girth, estimated to be 1,400 years old, which blew down in 1990.

The route continues along the Saxon named Short and Long Lythes (meadows), now owned by the National Trust, which run along the Oakhanger Stream Valley. The footpath emerges into a lovely meadow, grazed by Appaloosa ponies, with two lakes which support a wealth of wildlife, including swans and majestic grey heron. In order to avoid two stiles, the route diverts to the north of Coombe Wood and then follows a farm track for a short section before crossing the valley at Priory Farm (the site of the former Selborne Priory) and returning along a woodland footpath through the magnificent beech trees of Dorton Woods, with views over The Lythes from the opposite side of the valley.

Walk description

S. Leave the car park passing the Selborne Arms onto the B3006 and turn left signed 'Gilbert Whites House'. Continue through the village past the post office on your left and The Queens Inn on your right, then turn right before reaching The Selborne Gallery (opposite Gilbert Whites House) to follow a paved footpath through the Plestor (village green) towards an information board at the entrance to the church yard.

1. Go through metal gates into the church yard and continue along a paved footpath to a wooden kissing gate ahead (obstacle 1). Lift the little gate off its hinges to go through – please remember to replace the gate afterwards. There's an information board on your left describing the Lythes.
    Follow the footpath down the hill, across the meadow to a wooden foot bridge (obstacle 2). Lift your pushchair over the low barrier and cross the footbridge. Continue along the footpath along The Short Lythe, then after 200 yards go through a wooden kissing gate.

2. Follow the footpath round to the right to go through another wooden kissing gate, entering Long Lythe. Continue along a gravel path and up into a woodland. Follow the footpath along the picturesque Oakhanger Stream Valley and, after 525 yards, at the end of the wooded section, go through another wooden kissing gate to leave the Lythes and to enter a pretty grass meadow with views over two lakes.

3. Follow a footpath across the middle of the meadow, which is home to a small group of Appaloosa ponies. Continue along the length of the lake on your right, then turn left in front of a second little lake to continue around the edge of the field to a metal gate ahead.
    The path goes over a footbridge and through a kissing gate to the left which is unsuitable for pushchairs, so continue straight on through the metal gate. Then continue straight on up the slope to the top right hand corner of the field.

4. Turn right to go through a metal gate to the right of a wooden stile (lift a loop of metal wire over the gate post to open the gate), then follow a gravel footpath along the top of Coombe Woods.

5. After 245 yards, at the end of this path, go through another metal gate to enter a grass field. Follow a footpath up the slope to cross this field, passing a fenced

pond on your left. This path can be uneven in places. At the top corner of the field, go through a metal gate next to a wooden stile to enter the woods.

6. Immediately turn right onto a farm track. This track is uneven for a short section and is muddy in winter months; it also has some deep tyre ruts early on. After 240 yards the track bends to the left, with another deep tyre rut on the right. Then, after a further 165 yards, continue past two metal kissing gates, one on each side of the track.

7. Continue along the track as it bends left, then cross a stream over a concrete bridge with white railings. Keep right to follow the track around Priory Farm yard on your left and a lake on your right. Then bear right onto a minor road. After 35 yards, turn right down a gravel track signed 'Right of Way' passing a bungalow on your left.

8. After 85 yards, at the end of the track, go through a metal gate into a field. Continue straight on along the left hand edge of this field (this track can be uneven).

9. After 400 yards go through a metal bridleway gate into Great Dorton Woods. Follow the woodland path back along Oakhanger Stream Valley, with views of the Lythes to your right.

Appaloosa ponies taking shade by the lake

10. After just over 0.3 miles the path becomes a track as you approach Selborne village. At the end of this track you'll come to a wooden gate which is padlocked. To the left of the gate there are 3 separate railway sleepers, each 6 inches high (obstacle 3). Lift your pushchair over each sleeper to access Huckers Lane on the other side. Follow the lane up a hill.

11. After 400 yards, turn left onto the B3006 next to The Queens Inn (on your right). Cross over to make use of the pavement and follow the road back past the post office to The Selborne Arms. Turn right immediately after The Selborne Arms, into the village car park to complete the walk.

Refreshments

The Queens Hotel
High Street, Selborne, Alton GU34 3JJ
The Queens Hotel is a beautiful hotel and restaurant providing tea and coffee as well as lunch and evening meals.
www.selborne.parish.hants.gov.uk/village.html

Local attractions

Jane Austen's House Museum
Chawton, Alton GU34 1SD
The novelist Jane Austen is known worldwide for her popular novels describing the society of pre-industrial England. She spent the last eight years of her life, and wrote some of her best work, at Chawton in the 17th century house which is now preserved in her memory.
www.jane-austens-house-museum.org.uk

21. Ludshott Common and Waggoner's Wells

Distance	4.3 miles (6.9km)	Time taken	2 hours 30 mins
Grade	★★★★	Postcode	GU26 6JG
Grid Ref	SU852358	Total climb	280 ft (85m)
Map	Ordnance Survey Explorer Map: 1:25000 scale - Sheet 133		
Terrain	Sandy tracks, gravel tracks, wide woodland paths and Waggoner's Wells Lane, which is tarmac. The walk has level sections but also includes a number of fairly steep hills		
Obstacles	None		
Parking	Park at Ludshott Common off the B3002, Headley Road. The car park is situated 600 yards North West of Applegarth Farm Shop, 1 mile from Grayshott. Alternate parking is located at the end of Waggoner's Wells Lane (post code GU26 6DT, Grid Ref. SU862344). If you park here the walk can be started at point 14		

Much of the landscape in this tranquil corner of Hampshire is a patchwork of purple heather, yellow gorse and bracken covered heathland and deep wooded valleys created by tiny streams. This walk starts at Ludshott Common, which is one of the largest remaining areas of heathland in East Hampshire; a vast expanse of heathland and mixed deciduous woodland with far-reaching views from a number of vantage points.

In the Second World War the common was used as a training ground and over one hundred huts were erected to accommodate soldiers. After the war they were used for civilian housing until they were bulldozed in the early 1960s. Since then the area has been gradually reverting back to nature, although a number of garden species still persist, such as apple trees, rose bushes and privet hedges. The common is now designated a Site of Special Scientific Interest and Special Protection Area because of its wildlife, such as butterflies, damselflies and spiders; a diversity of birds, including in summer months the rare Dartford warbler, woodlark and nightjar; elusive deer and majestic birds of prey.

The writer Flora Thompson enjoyed exploring the common and undertook long rambles, during which she took detailed notes of nature and the changing seasons, which were published in the 1920s as short stories in a magazine called *The Catholic Fireside*, and later as a book entitled *The Peverel Papers*.

Heathland views at Ludshott Common

From the common the route descends to the stunning stream fed ponds at Waggoner's Wells, which were formed by the construction of a chain of dams in 1615, by Henry Hooke, it is thought for his iron foundry. There was a thriving iron industry in the area during the 17th century, although the ponds appear never to have actually been used for iron production.

The three ponds and surrounding mature beech woods are now a popular beauty spot owned by the National Trust and are important for wildlife, indeed the ponds contain a variety of fish and are home to kingfisher, coot, swans and other wildfowl. Lord Alfred Tennyson, Poet Laureate during much of Queen Victoria's reign, was known to walk beside these lakes, and wrote his famous short ode *Flower in the Crannied Wall*, in 1863, after pulling a flower from one of the crevices at the wishing well towards the valley bottom. His words are now etched in stone next to the wishing well.

Walk Description

S. From Ludshott Common car park follow a wide sandy path just to the left of a National Trust notice board. After 50 yards, continue straight on at a wide crossing of tracks.

1. After a further 35 yards, at a fork in the path, turn left and continue along the footpath as it gently descends. After 235 yards, continue straight on past a

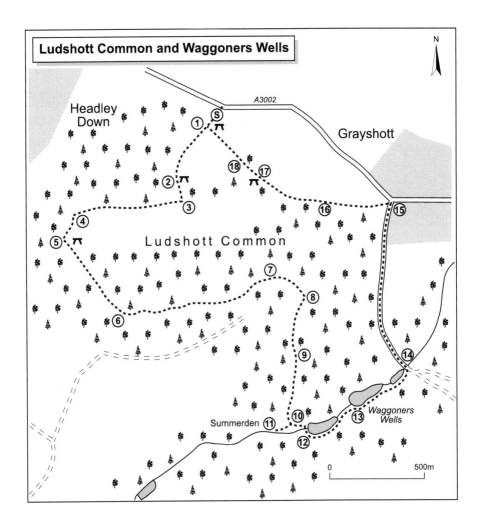

low slung branch (take care as the path now runs along sloping ground to the side of the original path to avoid the branch).

2. After a further 100 yards, pass a bench on your left with far reaching views over the common to your right. Follow the footpath round to the left and then down a short slope.

3. After another 25 yards, turn right at a junction to follow a sandy track through heathland.

4. Then, after 630 yards, at a fork in the path, turn left to cut the corner and, after another 40 yards, turn left to follow an uneven footpath up a hill.

5. After 150 yards, at a junction, turn left onto a bridleway. Then after another 55 yards, you'll reach a crossing of tracks, where there's a bench behind your left shoulder conveniently placed if you wish to enjoy the lovely views. From the bench cross the track and bear slightly right to rejoin the route. Continue straight on with a wooded area on your right and open heath on your left. After 150 yards, continue down a hill and cross a footpath then push up a small rise.

6. After another 275 yards, continue straight on past a turning into the woods on your right. Continue along the track with the woods on your right, then after 585 yards continue straight on where a path crosses the track on a diagonal.

7. After a further 445 yards, at a crossing of 5 tracks, take the third path from the left, or second from the right, to continue straight on along a grass track. Then, after 140 yards, bear left at a fork.

8. After another 95 yards, turn right onto a gravel track. Then, after 130 yards, at a fork in the track bear left, signed 'Summerden' and, after 95 yards, continue straight on as a bridleway crosses your way.

9. After 190 yards, keep right as the track forks before descending a stony slope. After a further 190 yards, continue straight on past a track joining from the left. After another 160 yards, pass a parking area in the trees on your right, and then bear left to go up a little slope and, after 25 yards, pass a path sloping sharply away on your right.

10. After 85 yards, at a junction, turn sharp right to visit the Tennyson wishing well. Walk along the valley with a stream below on your left. After 85 yards, pass steps up to Summerden House, then immediately bear left to go down a slope. At the bottom of the slope continue a little further, until you're nearly past the house above and you'll reach a small stone built wishing well with a run off channel across the path.

11. After making your wishes retrace your steps back up the slope. Bear right by the wooden steps and continue along the valley with the stream on your right. After 85 yards, pass the turning previously used and continue along the footpath to a wooden fence on your right and elaborate exposed roots in the bank on your left. Turn right to cross a wooden footbridge at the bottom of the first of the three lakes known as Wagoner's Wells.

12. Continue straight on to walk along the edge of the lake and, after 35 yards, turn left to continue around the lake. After another 285 yards, continue

straight on past a wooden platform over the out flow from the second lake. Continue along the footpath with the lake on your left.

13. After 50 yards, pass a footpath fingerpost on your left, then after a further 140 yards bear right at a fork to walk on slightly higher ground. After 20 yards bear slightly right just after a tree stump, then follow the path round to the left. After a further 150 yards pass a National Trust notice board on your right, then keep left to follow the path for a further 100 yards to the road.

14. Turn left onto Wagoner's Wells Road and, after 60 yards, cross a shallow ford (there's a footbridge on the right if you prefer). Follow the road up a long hill with Yaffles Wood on your left.

15. After 1050 yards, just before Headley Road, turn left onto a concrete drive, signed 'The Dower House'. Then, in 60 yards, pass The Dower House entrance on your right and continue for a further 35 yards, then turn right through wooden posts onto a bridleway.

16. After 400 yards, continue straight on past a bridleway on your left and a path through a fence line on your right. After a further 235 yards, at a junction, turn right to follow a sand/gravel track up a short hill.

The picturesque Waggoner's Wells

17. Then, after 160 yards, continue past another track and then a half log bench, both on your left. Continue down a slope and, after 75 yards, at a crossing of tracks, continue straight on and up another slope.

18. After a further 25 yards, pass a footpath on your left and continue up a hill. Then, after 325 yards, with a bench on your right, at a crossing of tracks, turn right to return to the parking area at the starting point.

Short Cut from point 7 (to avoid the hilly section down to Waggoner's Wells)
At the junction of five paths take the first path on the left. Follow this path for 350 yards, then at the bottom of a short slope turn right onto a wider path. After 70 yards, continue straight on at a crossing of paths, and after another 85 yards, follow the gravel track as it turns left up a short slope to rejoin the route at point 17. Distance of shortened walk: 2.25 miles; total climb: 148 ft.

Refreshments

Applegarth Farm Shop and Deli
Applegarth Farm, Headley Road, Grayshott GU26 6JL
Applegarth Farm Shop also features a deli, restaurant, children's play garden and potting shed. It's ideal for after-walk refreshments or to pick up a readymade picnic for your walk.
www.applegarthfarm.co.uk

Local Attractions

Grayshott Pottery and Café
Grayshott Pottery, School Road, Grayshott GU26 6LR
Grayshott Pottery has been making English stoneware since 1956. During your visit you can experience various pottery processes from traditional hand throwing to the modern hydraulic presses.
www.grayshottpottery.co.uk

Devils Punch Bowl and Hindhead Commons
Devils Punchbowl Café, London Road, Hindhead GU26 6AG
Owned by the National Trust, the Devil's Punch Bowl is a remarkable natural basin. It's Europe's largest spring-eroded valley. The stunning scenery of the Devil's Punch Bowl and Hindhead Commons can be enjoyed from the viewpoint 50 yards from the Devil's Punch Bowl Café.
www.visitsurrey.com/site/things-to-do/devils-punch-bowl-hindhead-commons-p46353

22. Alice Holt Forest

Distance	3 miles (4.9km)	Time taken	1 hour 15 mins
Grade	★★	Postcode	GU10 4LS
Grid Ref	SU810420	Total climb	150 ft (46m)
Map	Ordnance Survey Explorer Map: 1:25000 scale - Sheet 145		
Terrain	Gravel tracks and some paths		
Obstacles	None		
Parking	Alice Holt Forest Centre is off the A325, 5 miles South West of Farnham. At The Halfway House Pub on the A325, turn off the main road following signs for Alice Holt Forest. The entrance is 300 yards along this road on the left. There's a large onsite parking area which costs around £1 per hour (at the time of going to press)		

Alice Holt is an ancient forest, continuously wooded since trees first colonised the area after the last Ice Age. Early man lived on this site, as evidenced by finds of flint tools, some of which date back to the Palaeolithic, before the forest had established. Although the majority of finds are from the Mesolithic Age (up until 5,500 years ago), there are also more recent Neolithic and Bronze Age finds. In Roman times Gault Clay found in the forest was used to make a utilitarian ceramic, now known as 'Alice Holt Ware', and parts of the forest are thickly scattered with broken reject pots and blackened earth where the kilns once stood.

It's likely that the name Alice Holt is derived from 'Aelfsige's Holt' after Aelfsige, a Bishop of Winchester who preserved the forest for hunting in Anglo-Saxon times. In Medieval times, after the Norman conquest of 1066, the forest became a Royal Forest, protected by forest laws. In the late 14th century King Richard II used oak from the forest for the building of the roof of Westminster Hall.

During the 18th and 19th centuries Alice Holt oak trees supplied timber for navy ships and, in 1812, parliament passed an 'Act for The Better Cultivation of Navy Timber in The Forest of Alice Holt', which led to the ancient oaks being felled and replanted. Many magnificent, tall straight oaks survive from these plantings and others have been used in notable structures including the reconstruction of Shakespeare's Globe Theatre in London. Towards the end of the 19th Century the Crown Estate began introducing conifers (mainly Scots pine and larch). Then, in 1924, the Forestry Commission acquired the forest, which led to further oak being replaced with Corsican Pine to supply post war demands. This trend has now reversed and, as conifers are felled, broadleaved woodland is returning both through natural regeneration and planting of native species.

The forest is now designated as a Site of Interest for Nature Conservation, being a haven for a diversity of wildlife including rarities such as dormice, nocturnal nightjars (which can be seen hawking for food at dusk and dawn), hobbies (a fairly small, very swift falcon with long, narrow wings) and the magnificent and elusive purple emperor butterfly. In 2012 the forest will benefit from further protection afforded by its inclusion in the new South Downs National Park.

The forest has a wide range of facilities, including cycle hire, play areas and an extensive network of paths and tracks. A leaflet containing a map of the forest and showing five

Woodpecker giant play sculpture

way marked trails (not all suitable for pushchairs) can be obtained from stands in the forest car park.

The route described here initially follows the 'Family Cycle Trail' though the eastern side of the forest, then diverts onto a bridleway to join the 'Lodge Pond Trail' near the picturesque Lodge Pond. The final leg incorporates most of the 'Habitat Trail' with its giant play sculptures, which are suitable for toddlers to explore under supervision. The route then finishes past 'Go Ape' where older children (yes I mean dad) can be entertained whilst you're walking.

Walk Description

S. Starting from the cycle hire facility, with the café ahead to your right, turn left down the tarmac road. Then, after 10 yards, turn right down a gravel track signed 'Family Cycle Trail'. The first part of the walk follows this trail; it's marked with green cycle badges.

1. After 500 yards, continue straight across at a crossing of tracks. Then, after another 425 yards, keep straight on at a junction and continue along the track as it rises gently through the woods.

2. Then, after 600 yards, follow the track as it bends left, and after a further 500 yards, at the top of a hill, follow the track as it bends sharply to the left (cycle trail marker 17 and 18). Continue up a reasonably steep hill, passing a picnic area on your left.

3. At a junction of tracks (cycle trail marker 20), turn right. Then, after 175 yards, turn left at a junction of tracks to follow a bridle path through trees (leaving the cycle route). If the bridlepath is muddy continue along the cycle trail to marker 22 and turn right to marker 23.

4. At the end of the bridlepath, cross over a gravel track on an angle, to join a smaller gravel track (joining 'Lodge Pond Trail').

5. At a junction, cross a gravel track and follow a grass footpath towards the lake. Then, at the next junction, turn left to follow a footpath along the lakeside. After 100 yards, take the left fork to follow a footpath angled slightly away from the lake to a picnic area. Cross the picnic area towards a parking area. At a gravel track turn right to rejoin the cycle trail (cycle trail marker 25). Cross the parking area diagonally (there are portable toilets here) to follow a gravel track and turn right at marker 23 (joining 'Lodge Pond Trail').

Forest Lodge Café at Alice Holt

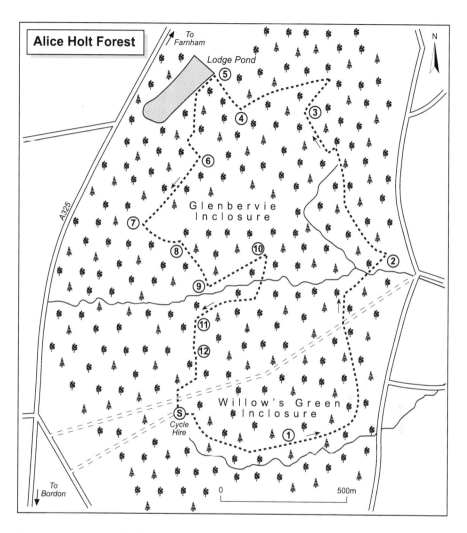

6. At a junction with the main track, turn right.

7. Then, after 375 yards, (just after cycle trail marker 30) turn left. After 100 yards, at a crossing of footpaths, continue straight on to follow the 'Lodge Pond Trail'.

8. After 75 yards, turn right to follow a footpath down to the Heritage Trail (not signed). This short section is a little bumpy (and can get muddy in winter months).

9. After 150 yards, at the end of the footpath turn left, with a huge owl sculpture on your right. Follow a gravel track, passing a spotted woodpecker sculpture and then a butterfly and bat sculpture, and continue over a large wooden bridge (look out for carved lizards on the bridge).

10. Immediately after the bridge at a crossing of tracks, turn right to walk down a hill, and then at a junction of gravel tracks turn right to pass a giants pencil sculpture on your right and continue along the Habitat Trail.

11. At the next crossing of tracks, turn left up a gentle hill. Then bear right at a fork in the path (next to a 'hidey hole' post) to go past a wooden bench.

12. Follow the path up a short hill to a tall totem pole next to 'Go Ape'. Continue along the track to cross the parking area. Then bear left to return to the starting point.

Refreshments

Alice Holt Forest Café
Alice Holt Forest, Farnham GU10 4LS
Alice Holt Forest Café serves a wide range of freshly prepared food and Fair Trade coffee and tea.
www.forestfoodcaterers.co.uk

Local Attractions

Go Ape
Alice Holt, Bucks Horn Oak, Nr Farnham GU10 4LS
If you're itching to swing through the trees, take your tribe to Go Ape for an outdoor, tree-top adventure and let out your inner monkey. Before you can head into the canopy, you'll need to be at least 10 years old and 4ft 7in. Liking bananas helps, but it's not essential.
www.goape.co.uk

Bird World
Holt Pound, Farnham GU10 4LD
Birdworld is one of the largest bird parks in the country. From a huge Ostrich to tiny Sunbirds, Penguins, Owls, Parrots, Waterfowl and many other colourful species, they have amazing birds from all around the world. On top of that, Birdworld is also home to the Jenny Wren Farm and Underwater World. There's a busy schedule of daily events.
www.birdworld.co.uk

23. Weston Common and Weston Patrick

Distance	4.5 miles (7.3km)	Time taken	2 hours
Grade	★★★★★	Postcode	GU34 5SU
Grid Ref	SU696439	Total climb	285 ft (87m)
Map	Ordnance Survey Explorer Map: 1:25000 scale - Sheet 144		
Terrain	Woodland tracks and paths, and a short section of country road. The first leg of this route is along grass tracks which can get a little muddy during the winter; a short section of the track, after Weston Patrick at Case Green, gets water logged in winter months (however it's possible to push your pushchair along the verge); and a short section of the footpath, just before re-entering Weston Wood is a bit awkward due to deep tyre ruts. This is a lovely walk if you have an all-terrain pushchair and don't mind short sections of muddy or rutted tracks		
Obstacles	None		
Parking	Turn eastward off the A339 between Basingstoke and Alton, just north of Lasham village, onto The Avenue. After 1.5 miles, just before The Avenue Nursery, turn left onto a woodland drive, which is shared with Humbly Grove Oil Field, then after 125 yards turn right in to Weston Wood parking area		

Weston Common is a 168 acre mixed deciduous woodland situated in a gently undulating landscape. It contains a number of archaeological features, including the Park Pale boundary that would have been used to keep grazing livestock in the wooded common and out of the Great Park. The wood still bears the hallmark funnel shape of a wooded common. The wood is not commercially managed at present and has a full complement of woodland wildlife.

Perhaps unexpectedly for a wooded common, Weston Common is home to Humbly Grove oil field, which was discovered in 1980 and began production in 1984, with up to 1,000 barrels a day of crude oil being piped to a terminal near Alton. However the site is obscured by trees and not particularly visible from this walk, other than the sign at the entrance.

This route starts with a more or less straight line walk of one mile along a grass bridleway, alongside Park Pale, between Great Park and Closedown Wood, to Closedown House. It then turns left, passing Holding Corner, which was originally an interim stock holding area, to walk along a lovely bridleway known as Long

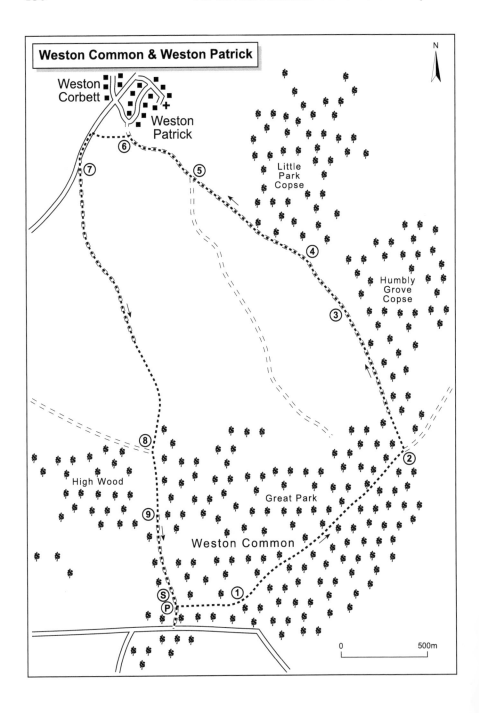

Weston Common & Weston Patrick

Weston Corbett

Weston Patrick

Little Park Copse

Humbly Grove Copse

High Wood

Great Park

Weston Common

N

0   500m

Lane, with Humbly Grove Copse and then Little Park Copse to your right. After another mile the track leaves its wooded landscape to cross open farmland towards Weston Patrick half a mile ahead.

The name Weston Patrick is probably derived from Patrick de Chaworth who owned the manor during the 13th century. The walk doesn't actually enter the village but bears left to walk briefly along a country road before climbing gently along a farm track and then back through Weston Common, passing a large disused pit, before reaching the entrance to the woods at the starting point.

Walk Description

S. From the parking area, walk away from the tarmac drive to go around a metal barrier to follow a gravel track into Weston Common Woods. After 250 yards, pass a corrugated iron shed and several timber stacks on your left.

1. After a further 75 yards, bear left at a fork, then after 145 yards continue straight on at a crossing of tracks. After another 375 yards, pass a track on your left and, after 165 yards, continue under telephone lines. This section is muddy during winter months. After 225 yards pass a track on your right, with Closedown Wood to your right. After another 345 yards pass another turning to your right.

2. After a further 300 yards, in front of a metal barrier and house beyond, turn left, then immediately bear right at a fork in the path to go between two concrete pillars onto a bridleway. Follow the bridleway alongside a trimmed hedge to your right. After 245 yards, as the path emerges from the woods, continue straight on along the right hand edge of an arable field, now with Holding Corner and later Humbly Grove Copse to your right. After 350 yards, continue on up a hill, passing a turning on your right marked with a small 'Wildlife Conservation Area – Do Not Enter' notice pinned to a large oak tree.

3. After a further 420 yards, in the corner of the field, follow a track round to the right into trees. Then, after just 20 yards, turn left to follow another track along a corridor of trees. After another 145 yards, as the track turns left, continue straight on to follow a pretty foot path under an arch of trees.

4. After 185 yards, at a junction, bear left to join a track. Follow the track with arable fields to your left and Little Park Copse on your right. After 415 yards follow the track as it turns right, passing a turning to your left. Continue down the hill passing a productive blackberry bush on your right and, after 115 yards, continue under electricity cables.

5. After 415 yards, at a junction, bear right onto a gravel farm track with a hedge on both sides. Then, after 120 yards, as the track turns to the right, continue

straight on to follow a footpath under an arch of trees. Follow this path down a hill then, after 325 yards, continue straight on past a footpath on your right.

6. After another 95 yards, with a metal gate (to a pony paddock) on your right, turn left and push up a short slope to join a footpath around the right hand edge of an arable field. Continue down a slope, for 250 yards, to exit the field at the bottom corner and turn left onto the main road to the Weston Patrick. Take care along the road as traffic can travel quite quickly along this section (walk on the outside of the right hand bend to maximise your visibility to oncoming traffic).

7. After 200 yards, bear left onto a gravel track (next to a telegraph pole). Follow this track adjacent to the road and then, before it completes its loop back to the road, turn left onto a farm track. The first 45 yards can be waterlogged in winter months, however it's possible to push your pushchair along the right hand verge (taking care not to slip into the water logged wheel ruts). Continue along this farm track, then after 500 yards, where the track forks, turn left under telegraph lines onto a grass track.

8. After 1,545 yards (0.85 miles), continue straight on past a track on your right, marked with a finger post to your left. The track is rutted for the next 250 yards but becomes easier for the remaining 150 yards to Weston Wood ahead.

9. Continue straight on into the woods and follow the woodland track passing the oil field, unseen to your left. Then, after 350 yards, pass a large pit on your right. After a further 315 yards, continue straight on alongside a post and rail fence, then turn left into the parking area at the starting point.

Look to the skies above the bridleway leading down to Weston Patrick

Refreshments

The Royal Oak
Lasham Village GU34 5SJ
Cosy log fires for the winter months and spacious, beautifully maintained gardens for when the sun shines! This pub offers quality, locally purchased food including fresh fish dishes. Children are most welcome.
www.royaloak.uk.com/index.html

Local attractions

The Mid Hants Railway 'Watercress Line'
Station Road, Alton GU34 2PZ
Sit back, relax, and watch mile after mile of beautiful Hampshire countryside pass you by. The soothing sounds of the steam engine with the beat of the exhaust can be heard over the clickety clack of the wheels passing over the rails. The sedate pace of life can be enjoyed watching the trains go by at one of the peaceful and picturesque stations.
www.watercressline.co.uk

Lasham Gliding
The Avenue, Lasham Airfield, Alton GU34 5SS
Lasham Gliding offers trial 'one off' lessons consisting of a single flight gliding lesson. There's an onsite restaurant and bar open every day throughout the summer for meals and snacks.
www.lashamgliding.co.uk

24. Caesars Camp

Distance	3.6 miles (5.8km)	Time taken	2 hours
Grade	★★★★	Postcode	GU10 5BY
Grid Ref	SU831510	Total climb	290 ft (88m)
Map	Ordnance Survey Explorer Map: 1:25000 scale – Sheet 145		
Terrain	Gravel tracks and paths, some of which are fairly stony. The walk has level sections but also includes a number of steep climbs and descents		
Obstacles	None		
Parking	The parking area is situated 2 miles from the centre of Aldershot. Head West out of Aldershot on the A323, Wellington Avenue. At the roundabout (junction with the A325, Farnborough Road), take the 2nd exit onto Wellesley Road. Continue onto Bourley Road, then after 1.3 miles the parking area will be on your right		

This is a lovely, albeit fairly strenuous walk, on military gravel tracks. Starting across one of the army camping grounds, this route continues through the mature mixed coniferous forest of Parkhurst Hill, passing a small reservoir, and then across Bourley Bottom to another pretty reservoir. These reservoirs adjoin the water works and contribute to the local water supply but nevertheless are teeming with wildlife. The route then climbs up a reasonably steep stony footpath onto Caesar's Camp. Despite the name, Caesar's Camp is in fact the site of an Iron Age hill fort built around 2500-2700 years ago. The entire hill top is encircled with double ramparts creating what would have been a formidable defence. The route crosses the undulating ramparts to gain access to the summit then follows

Heathland views below Caesars Camp

the western edge with far reaching views over the surrounding forest and countryside beyond. At the north eastern corner of the summit there is a cluster of large trees and a wooden bench from which to appreciate the far reaching views towards Aldershot.

The route continues down Windy Gap Hill along a lightly undulating but straight section of gravel track, with open views over the surrounding heathland, then joins a tarmac drive through mixed deciduous woodland to cross Bourley road. Once over the road the route continues along similar gravel tracks over undulating heathland, with a climb up Jubilee Hill, before passing army camping grounds and returning to the parking area at the starting point.

The whole area is owned by the Ministry of Defence for training but it's also a great place for wildlife because of its open heathland, forests and reservoirs. In the summer you can see the nocturnal nightjar and in the autumn fly agaric toadstools are dotted around the site. The area is managed by Hampshire Wildlife Trust who graze cattle on the site to keep the vegetation under check for conservation purposes. Keep a look out for birds of prey, such as kestrel hunting over the heathland.

If you're weekend walking in early October you may see a number of very weary runners completing the 50 or 100 mile 'Caesar's Camp Endurance Runs'. The course is a repeated 10 mile loop with a 1,520 foot climb on each lap. It's a qualifier for 'The North Face Ultra Trail Du Mont-Blanc', if you're interested in competing.

Walk description

S. From the entrance of the parking area, cross Bourley Road with great care as it can be busy, then go around a metal barrier, next to an MOD sign, into an open field (used as an army camping ground). Follow a gravel track along the left hand edge of the field, then after 100 yards bear right to follow a grass path diagonally across the field.

1. At the corner of the field bear right to follow a gravel track under oak trees. Then bear left to follow a path across a corner and turn left onto a gravel track. After 35 yards, at a crossing of tracks, continue straight on.

2. After another 165 yards continue straight on past a reservoir to your left, then after a further 240 yards, at the junction, follow the track round to the left. This track passes Beacon Hill through the trees to your right.

3. After 225 yards, continue straight on at the crossing of tracks. Then after another 175 yards pass a grass track on your right and follow the track as it bears left and continues down a gentle slope.

4. After 125 yards, at a crossing of tracks (with 2 grass tracks ahead), turn left to follow a gravel track. After 100 yards pass a pretty reservoir on your left,

then after a further 65 yards, where a footpath gives you a lovely view of the reservoir, turn right away from the reservoir onto a stony track. After 70 yards, continue straight on to join another track merging from the left.

5. Follow the track up hill, then after 375 yards, at a junction (with the Iron Age fort on top of the hill in front of you) turn right to follow a track along a fence line. After 35 yards, turn left to go through a large metal kissing gate, then push up a steep stony hill. This path can be a little wet due to seepage from natural springs.

6. After 175 yards, at the top of the hill, turn left at the crossing of tracks to enter the fort. Follow the footpath as it undulates over the ramparts, then at the junction (just inside the fort) turn left to follow a gravel track around the summit, with great views over the forest below and beyond. After 200 yards continue straight on as a track merges from the right. From this point you'll be able to see a large white dome of a covered reservoir at the foot of the hill, and a bit further round the views will include Farnborough Airfield.

7. After another 375 yards, at a cluster of large trees, there are a couple of wooden benches with far reaching views over Farnborough and Aldershot. The

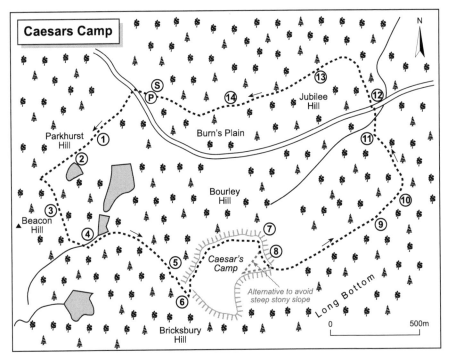

area under the trees here offers potential for a picnic but is used by cattle so beware of deposits.

At this point the paths down from the fort are all very steep, but if you continue around the top of the fort the descent becomes easier. After 80 yards from the cluster of large trees, at a fork, bear left to keep the steep slope on your left.

8. Then, after a further 100 yards, continue straight on to head down a stony gully. Take care making your way down this steep little hill as the cobble sized stones are loose. At the bottom of the gully, turn left onto a gravel track.

[If you don't fancy this stony route down, then continue past the top of the gully to follow a track to your right. After 135 yards turn left to join another gravel track, then continue down a short slope and, after 25 yards, turn left at a junction. Follow a gravel track down hill beneath the Iron Age ramparts to your left. After 315 yards, keep left at a fork to stay on higher ground, then after a further 35 yards continue straight on passing the stony hill on your left to rejoin the route].

9. Continue along this track as it gradually descends and, after 600 yards at a junction of a number of tracks, continue straight on to climb onto a large mound. At this point it's worth pausing to take in the view of the Iron Age Fort behind you.

10. After another 175 yards at a junction in front of a conifer wood, turn left onto a tarmac track. Follow this track as it sweeps left and continues downhill. After 225 yards at the crossing of tracks, continue straight on.

11. Then after a further 185 yards, at a junction, turn right, with a red brick shed on your right. Follow this tarmac track for 155 yards to go over a cattle grid (or through the gate to the left) and around a metal barrier.

12. Cross over Bourley Road with care, bearing slightly left into a concrete parking area. Cross the parking area, then go around a metal barrier and continue along a gravel track. After 215 yards, at a fork bear left to follow the track up a slope to Jubilee Hill.

13. Keep left, then after 335 yards, at a crossing of tracks at the top of a hill, continue straight on following this undulating track. After a further 350 yards, after climbing another steep little hill to an open area, continue straight on at a crossing of tracks. Then, after 85 yards, at the bottom of a steep hill, as the track turns to the right, continue straight on up another steep hill.

14. After 125 yards, continue straight on at a crossing of tracks. Then, after a further 175 yards, at a junction turn right into trees, then walk alongside a

camping ground on your left. Follow this track around the camping ground for 315 yards and back to the parking area at the starting point.

Refreshments

The Horns (3 miles)
The Horns, Bowling Alley, Crondall, Farnham GU10 5RJ
The Horns combines a traditional English rural pub feel with that of a country dining room, offering unpretentious locally sourced and homemade food at value for money prices.
www.thehorns.co.uk

Local attractions

The Wellington Statue (2 miles)
Round Hill, Wellesley Road, Aldershot GU11 1QA
Behind the Royal Garrison Church of All Saints, upon Round Hill, stands a great equestrian statue of the first Duke of Wellington mounted on his charger, Copenhagen. There's plenty of open space to run about or have a picnic beneath the statue.
www.ukattraction.com/southern-england/the-wellington-statue.htm

Sandy tracks near Bourley Hill

The Wellington Statue

Alpine Snowsports (3.5 miles)
Gallwey Road, Aldershot GU11 2DD
Alpine Snowsports has three ski slopes, the main slope is 110 meters long and two nursery areas are 75 meters long. All slopes are fully floodlit and have a mist system. There is a lower age limit of 4 years. Ample free parking, fully licensed bar and ski shop.
www.alpinesnowsports.co.uk

Aldershot Military Museum (4 miles)
Queens Avenue, Aldershot GU11 2LG
Aldershot Military Museum is based in one of only two surviving barrack bungalows built in North Camp in the 1890s. There are many different types of activity available; children will love the puzzle cubes and riding on a real tank, while adults might prefer the many uniforms, badges, medals, weapons and military vehicles on display.
www3.hants.gov.uk/aldershot-museum

25. Greywell and Odiham Castle

Distance	3.3 miles (5.3km)	Time taken	1 hour 30 mins
Grade	★ ★ ★	Postcode	RG29 1BY
Grid Ref	SU718513	Total climb	155 ft (47m)
Map	Ordnance Survey Explorer Map: 1:25000 scale - Sheet 144		
Terrain	Canal side and woodland footpaths, a short section of country road		
Obstacles	There are two obstacles on this walk where it's easier with two people to lift your pushchair. 1. To enter Butter Wood from Hook Road the footpath goes through a gap next to a metal barrier. Part of the gap is blocked with a small concrete block. Two people are needed to lift your pushchair over the block. If you're on your own it is recommended that you take your little one out before attempting to lift your pushchair over the block. 2. Towards the end of the walk, in Butter Wood, there's a narrow footbridge to cross (two railway sleepers wide, but only one sleeper long). This is easily negotiated with a 3-wheel pushchair by lifting the back wheels off the ground and pushing the pushchair across on its front wheel		
Parking	This walks start from The Fox and Goose Inn in Greywell. It's located just 1.5 miles from junction 5 of the M3. At the roundabout, take the exit onto the A287 heading to Farnham. After 0.2 miles, turn right onto Hook Road towards Greywell. Follow this road for 1 mile, then turn right into the pub car park just after the turning on your left to Odiham (Deptford Lane)		

This walk starts in the picturesque village of Greywell, a tiny settlement that offers a surprisingly remote and peaceful atmosphere given its proximity to the M3 motorway. The village comprises a number of houses and cottages of historical interest, many timber framed, and a 16th century inn. The church of 'St Mary the Virgin' lies a hundred yards or so south-east of the village centre. A large part of the church dates from the 12th century; around the Norman doorway are a dozen crosses carved by men from Greywell before they left to take part in the of Crusades.

The route leaves the village to walk alongside the tranquil Basingstoke Canal. Built in 1794 the canal was used to take shipments of timber, coal, grain, malt and a multitude of other goods from north Hampshire, through 29 locks in Surrey, to London. The construction of the railways led to a decline in the commercial popularity of the canal but it was used again in the First World War to move munitions, after which time it fell into disrepair. After restoration, it was again opened as a leisure amenity in 1991 and is now considered to be a linear country park, indeed much of the canal is now a Site of Special Scientific Interest. The clean spring water supplying the canal provides an ideal habitat for a wealth of wildlife, such as dragonflies, heron, moor hens, little grebe, mallards, swans, kingfishers, water voles and wagtails. The clear waters are great for aquatic plants and the banks have an abundance of flowers during summer months, attracting numerous butterflies. A disused section of the Basingstoke Canal which runs under Greywell Hill Park, along a tunnel of nearly a mile long, is home to large colonies of both Natterer's and Daubenton's bats, and is the largest bat roost in Britain.

After little over half a mile the route passes the impressive ruins of King John's Castle, also known as Odiham Castle, set back from the towpath it's a picturesque spot for a picnic. This fortified hunting lodge, built in 1212, was one of only three strongholds built for King John, to add to the ninety he already had at his disposal; the site was probably chosen because it lay halfway between Windsor and Winchester. In 1216 Prince Louis of France laid siege upon the stronghold in a claim to the English throne. His position was short lived, and he retreated within a year in response to forces loyal to King John's true successor, King Henry III.

The route continues along the canal to a swing bridge at Warnborough Green where there's often a pair of swans, with a family of signets in summer months. The route then crosses two fords to enter 'Bartley Heath and Warnborough Greens' which are managed by Hampshire Wildlife Trust. After a few yards along Hook Road, the route follows woodland tracks and footpaths through Butter Wood; a large ancient woodland which is commercially managed. The route passes temporary enclosures, erected on the advice of 'Natural England' to protect the re-growth of hazel coppice from deer browsing. It then continues along the line of the Greywell tunnel, although there is little evidence of the structure beneath, and emerges from the woodland into Greywell Hill Park, with views of the grand Greywell House, before following a footpath through a small wooded area back to the starting point.

Walk Description

S. Leave the pub car park and turn left onto The Street, then within a few yards turn right onto Deptford Lane, signed 'Odiham' and 'North Warnborough'. Almost immediately mount the curb on your left to join a footpath alongside the road, then bear left away from the road after 20 yards.

1. Follow this footpath to cross the end of Greywell Tunnel over the Basingstoke Canal, then after a few yards turn right in front of a metal gate to go down a

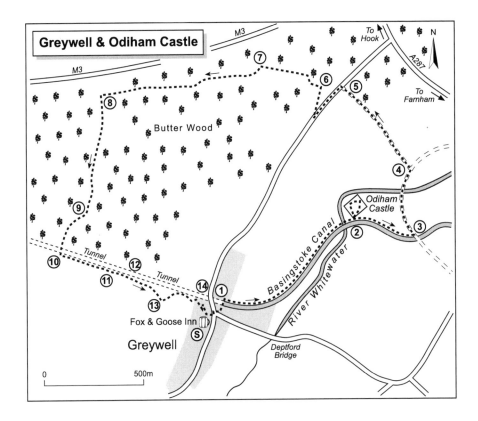

slope and walk along a gravel canal side path. There's a 'Basingstoke Canal and Greywell Tunnel' information board here.

2. Continue along the gravel path alongside the canal for 900 yards until you come to Odiham Castle on your left. The castle remains are worth a visit as part of this walk and provide a pretty spot for a picnic. From the castle turn left on to the canal side path to continue on your way.

3. After 360 yards, where a swing bridge crosses the canal, go around a wooden gate and turn left onto a road. After 225 yards continue straight on to cross a ford, using the pavement on the left. Then go through a small wooden gate to enter 'Bartley Heath and Warnborough Greens'. Continue along the road and after 65 yards cross another ford, again using the pavement on the left.

4. Then immediately turn left to go through a small wooden gate to the right of a cattle grid, signed 'Footpath'. Follow the road past houses and, after 75

yards, go through a small wooden gate. Turn right on to a grass track, then immediately turn left to follow a footpath into trees.

5. After 495 yards bear left to go through the smaller wooden gate to the left, then cross straight over Hook Road and turn left to walk along the roadside. After 150 yards, turn right to re-enter 'Bartley Heath and Warnborough Greens' and follow the tarmac track round to the right.

6. After 120 yards, just past a house, turn left. Follow the grass track into Butter Wood by going through a gap to the right of the metal barrier. There's a concrete block partially blocking the gap which you will need to lift your pushchair over (obstacle 1).

    After 55 yards take the right fork, passing a green 'Footpath Only' sign on your left and continue along the footpath, with a grass field through the trees on your left. The footpaths throughout Butter Wood are marked with a good supply of yellow arrows on footpath marker posts.

7. After a further 285 yards keep left at a fork, as indicated by a yellow arrow. Then, after another 35 yards, with a yellow footpath marker to your right, take the right fork to continue through the wood. After 195 yards, continue straight on at a crossing of paths, with a footpath marker post on your right.

The stunning ruins of King Johns Castle

After 100 yards, pass a track on your right and, after another 125 yards, just after a yellow arrow marker post, cross straight over a track. Then, after another 210 yards, continue straight on at a crossing of tracks and, after 215 yards, pass the first of two wooden sheds on your right.

8. After 35 yards, at a junction, turn left along a grass track to join a woodland track, heading directly away from the M3 motorway. After 75 yards, pass the top of a wide grass margin to your left, with a footpath marker post on your right. Then, after 115 yards, at a fork bear right off the woodland track, as indicated by a footpath marker.

   Continue past a temporary enclosure to your left. There is a shallow ditch and bank, marking an old boundary, to the right of the footpath along the length of this leg of the route.

   After 165 yards (immediately after a large oak tree on your left), continue straight on at a crossing of tracks, as indicated by a yellow arrow marker post.

9. After a further 315 yards, at the end of the temporary enclosure, turn right at a crossing of tracks, as indicated by a yellow arrow marker post. Then, after 30 yards, continue straight on past a track on your left and, after another 30 yards, bear left at a fork in the path, as indicated by a yellow arrow. Then, after 25 yards, turn left down a fairly steep grass hill. After 125 yards, at the bottom of the hill, bear slightly left to cross over a track and continue over a small wooden foot bridge (obstacle 2) as indicated by the yellow arrow.

10. After 55 yards, at a junction turn left onto a gravel bridleway and, in 100 yards, continue straight on at a crossing of tracks. Then, after 35 yards, continue straight over another crossing of tracks and head up a slight gradient.

11. After 175 yards, at the top of the slope, go through a wooden gate and continue straight on up a slope, passing a large oak tree on your right, then after 25 yards, bear slightly left towards a finger post standing under a large oak tree 50 yards ahead. Pause to take in the view of Greywell Hill House behind you.

12. From the large oak tree, bear slightly right to follow a footpath diagonally across the field to the bottom left hand corner.

13. After 200 yards, in the corner of the field, go through a black metal kissing gate (it's fairly tight for an all-terrain pushchair), then follow this pretty footpath down through the woodland. After 200 yards, at the bottom of a small slope, follow the path round to the left, passing footpath on your right.

14. After 25 yards turn right through a gap in the fence, and follow a short path into the back of the pub field. Cross the field to return to the starting point.

Refreshments

Fox and Goose Inn

The Street, Greywell, Hook RG29 1BY
This quaint 16th century country Inn
has a relaxed atmosphere, set in the
heart of this tranquil village. The pub
cuisine is mostly traditional English
fayre with the emphasis on homemade dishes. Children are welcome at
the pub all year round and there is
ample room for them to play in the
garden.
www.foxandgoosegreywell.co.uk

Local attractions

Odiham (King John's) Castle

Tunnel Lane, North Warnborough
RG29 1HQ
The route passes the ruins of King
John's castle. King John may have
decided on Odiham as a suitable site
for a castle on his visit to the town in
1204. Construction began in 1207 and
continued until 1214. In 1216, soon
after it was finished, the castle
suffered a two-week siege at the hands
of the French, but it flourished during
much of the 13th century, when it was
home to the de Montfort family.

A family of swans under the swing bridge at
Warnborough Green

www3.hants.gov.uk/hampshire-
countryside/odiham-castle.htm

Basingstoke Canal Boat Trips (2.3 miles)

Colt Hill, Odiham RG29 1HJ
Enjoy up to 2½ hours of gentle cruising through scenic North Hampshire,
observing a wide variety of plant and wild life, and a number of canal features.
Drinks and snacks are available on the boat.
www.s-h-c-c.co.uk

26. Basing, Crabtree Plantation and Black Dam Ponds

Distance	3.9 miles (6.3km)	Time taken	2 hours
Grade	★★	Postcode	RG24 8AE
Grid Ref	SU660530	Total climb	120 ft (37m)
Map	Ordnance Survey Explorer Map: 1:25000 scale - Sheet 144		
Terrain	All weather riverside paths, minor roads and grass footpaths. The walk is for the most part level but also includes some gentle gradients		
Obstacles	The route crosses the A30 at two points. The A30 can be busy so please don't attempt this crossing with walking toddlers and take great care crossing with your pushchair		
Parking	Park at Basing House Parking situated adjacent to The Millstone Public House off Barton's Lane. The entrance is on the right 0.2 miles after you turn onto Barton's Lane. Follow the drive towards the pub then turn right to access Basing House parking		

This route starts at The Millstone, an idyllic country pub, to walk along a pretty riverside footpath towards Basing House. Although there's an admission charge to visit Basing House itself, there's no charge to go into the visitor centre which takes you past a magnificent Tudor Barn, the largest in Southern England. The route accommodates a visit to Basing House but can equally be undertaken without if time is limited.

The earliest visible features at Basing House today are the huge defensive ringworks and ditches of a castle built in the 12th century by the de Port family, who arrived during the Norman invasion of 1066. A new house was later built on the same site in 1535 by Sir William Paulet, the first Marques of Winchester. At the time it was the largest private house in England, with more than 360 rooms, and was frequented by the monarchs of the day. During the civil war, Basing House was attacked by Parliamentary troops several times, but it wasn't until an assault led by Oliver Cromwell in 1645 that the defences were breached and Basing House was destroyed by fire. Today little more than the foundations and cellars are left.

Leaving Basing House the route continues across the expansive Basingstoke Common. The original common was incorporated into War Memorial Park as part of the new town development and the current common was provided to replace the original. The common is grazed by cattle to conserve the diversity of meadow flora, which is awash with buttercups during summer months. From the common the route crosses the A30 to enter Crabtree Plantation through the grand, grade II listed, concrete pillared Bolton Arch, a remnant of the parks historical significance, and formerly the entrance to Hackwood Estate. The route then follows a surfaced footpath across open grassland, adjacent to mixed deciduous woodland of oak, sycamore, ash and horse chestnut. The south facing grassland is managed for its flowering plants which attracts significant numbers of butterflies of many varieties, but is also popular with dog walkers and kite fliers alike.

The walk continues through Black Dam Reserve and on to Black Dam ponds where there's a children's playground and a wildfowl feeding platform. There's an opportunity to walk around the ponds which provide a haven for wildlife, such as coots, swans, tufted ducks and kingfishers. The route then heads back via Basing Lime Pits, where there's a large play ground and picnic area. The walk continues past an Amphitheatre and back through Basingstoke Common then along Redbridge Lane, crossing Basingstoke canal over a red brick bridge. This bridge, typical of the 18th century design, is the only canal structure still visible west of Basing House, where there's a sizeable bridge just inside Garrison Gate.

Walk Description

S. From Basing House car park, follow the gravel pavement past a Basing House information board. Continue along the pavement in front of red brick buildings, then around a wooden barrier to cross the tarmac pub drive.

1. Almost immediately, in front of a wooden gate, turn right to go through a gap in a brick wall, following signs for Basing House visitor centre. Continue across the pub seating area to pass the entrance of Barton Mill Restaurant, then follow a footpath round to the right and over a bridge to cross the river. Follow a gravel path alongside the river, then after 85 yards continue under the tall arches of a railway bridge.

2. After another 125 yards you'll come to the entrance to Basing House visitor centre. Follow A) if you're visiting Basing House, or B) if you're not including the attraction as part of this walk.

A) If you intend to visit this attraction, turn left to cross a wooden footbridge, then bear right to go through a small wooden gate. Follow a footpath past a large Tudor Barn and continue to the visitor centre, where you can pay to visit Basing House.

Follow signs for 'House, Garden and Museum' across the yard, and continue to the road. Turn left onto the road, cross over once you're opposite the entrance to 'Garrison Gate' and follow the drive into the attraction. There's plenty to see here, but once you've finished make your way to the disabled parking area, to the rear of the walled garden, either through a gate below the museum or follow a track down the hill beneath the cannon.

Follow a gravel track from this parking area, passing a small stable block on your right. Then, after 195 yards, as the drive turns to the right, continue straight on to go through a metal kissing gate.

B) If you are not visiting Basing House then continue along the footpath alongside the river and, after 85 yards, turn left onto the road to walk along a red brick pavement. After 100 yards, where the road bends sharply left, turn right onto Redbridge Lane, then after 370 yards follow the road round to the left and continue across a redbrick bridge over Basingstoke Canal. At a junction turn left in front of wooden gates, onto a minor road. Then, after 120 yards, just before a bend in the road, turn right to go through a metal kissing gate.

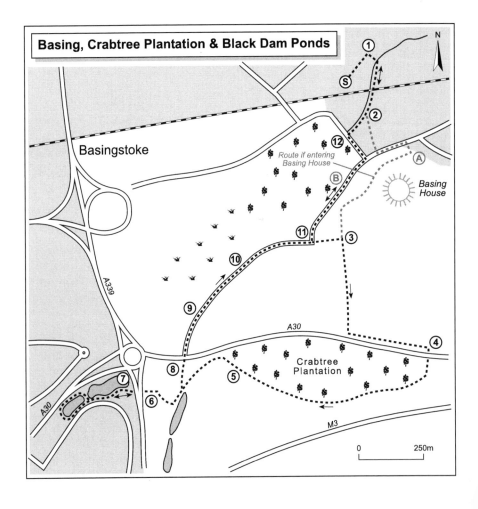

3. From the metal kissing gate, pass another metal kissing gate on your left and follow a footpath straight across the field, with a hedge line on your left. This field is Basingstoke Common; which is beautifully carpeted with buttercups in summer months. After 450 yards, before the A30 ahead, turn left to cross the hedge line and go through a metal kissing gate. Follow a grass footpath up a hill, walking in line with the electricity cables above.

4. After 340 yards, at the top if the hill, turn right to go through another metal kissing gate and to cross over the A30 (this is a fast road so cross with great care). Continue into Crabtree Plantation car park with a grand concrete entrance ahead. Cross the car park and push under a black barrier between the concrete pillars. Pass a black information board on your right and continue along the woodland path. After 35 yards, keep right to continue along a gravel path with the woods on your right and a hedge on your left.

5. Continue along this path, climbing a gentle hill and, in 575 yards, at the end of the woods, continue along the path as it curves down a hill. After 285 yards, at the bottom of the hill, follow the path as it curves to the left, passing a blue cycle route fingerpost. Then, after 85 yards, turn right, signed 'Black Dam Ponds'.

6. After 80 yards, pass a turning on your left and continue straight on to go through an underpass. Continue up the ramp and, after 25 yards, turn right to follow a footpath around a children's play area. As you approach the first pond, pass a wildfowl feeding platform on your right. This is a great spot to stop for a break, but once you've finished playing and feeding there's an option to take a brief walk around the ponds. If you prefer to continue on the main route go to point 7 below.

For a loop around Black Dam Ponds:

(a) Continue along the tarmac footpath with the first pond on your right, then after 135 yards turn right onto another path to walk under a willow tree between the first and second ponds. The ponds provide a haven for wildlife, particularly waterfowl including coots, tufted ducks and kingfishers.

(b) Follow the path around the second pond, passing an information board on your left. Then, after 260 yards, cross a wooden footbridge and immediately turn left. Then at a junction, in front of a road, turn left again.

(c) After 185 yards continue straight on, past the turning just taken, and retrace your steps back to the feeding platform.

7. From the feeding platform head back around the play ground, turning left to walk back under the underpass. After 25 yards, bear left at a fork next to a

Black Dam and Crabtree Nature Reserve information board. Then, after 85 yards, at a junction, turn left, signed 'Crabtree Plantation'. Continue for another 85 yards to the blue cycle route finger post.

8. Then turn left off the main path, signed 'Old Basing (via Redbridge Lane)'. Follow a narrow earth footpath up to the road, passing a metal gate on your right. Cross the A30, again with great care, and continue along Redbridge Lane.

9. After 200 yards turn right into 'Basing Lime Pits'. Cross the parking area and continue across a playground, keeping left to find a footpath through trees. Follow this path for 65 yards to pass a play train and duck under a little 'station' archway. Continue straight on to cross the play area, past monkey bars to exit the play area.

  Continue up a short slope towards an amphitheatre, but before reaching the top of the slope (which forms the side of the amphitheatre), turn left to go through a gateway into a parking area. Keep right through the parking area, then continue straight on, where the road turns left (down to the entrance of the car park), to go through a metal kissing gate.

10. Follow a grass footpath across an overgrown meadow to another metal kissing gate. Go through the gate then turn left to follow the left hand edge of

The feeding platform at Black Dam Ponds

Basingstoke Common. After 50 yards continue round the corner of the field, then after 230 yards pass a 'Basingstoke Canal Heritage Footpath' information board and wooden gates to continue around the edge of the field. After another 135 yards, just before a hedge line, turn left to go through a metal kissing gate, then turn left onto a minor road.

11. After 140 yards, at a junction, turn right onto Redbridge Lane to cross an old redbrick bridge over Basingstoke Canal. After 485 yards, at a junction with Basing Road, cross over to use the red brick pavement and turn left.

12. After 105 yards, before crossing a bridge, turn right to join a footpath with the river on your left. After 45 yards pass the entrance to Basing House visitor centre on your right. Continue along the riverside footpath for 285 yards, then cross a bridge and bear left to go through the pub seating area. Continue through a gap in the wall and then immediately turn left to cross the road and follow a gravel footpath in front of red brick buildings. Follow this path back to the parking area at the start of the walk.

Refreshments

The Millstone
The Millstone, Barton's Lane, Old Basing RG24 8AE
The Millstone is set within a conservation area near the historical Basing House. Enjoy delicious homemade food by the calming waters of the River Loddon. Barton's Mill restaurant next door offers excellent food in the traditional setting of the original watermill.
ww.millstoneoldbasing.co.uk/home.php

Local Attractions

Basing House
Basing House Visitor Centre, Basing Grange, The Street, Old Basing, Basingstoke RG24 7BH
The earliest visible features at Basing House today are the huge circular bank and defensive ditches of a castle built in the 1100s, also evident are the extensive cellars of a substantial house built in 1535 on the same plot. The site also includes a huge Tudor barn, a visitor centre, museum, walled Jacobean gardens and The Bothy tearoom.
www3.hants.gov.uk/basing-house

27. Morgaston Woods

Distance	1.7 miles (2.7km)	Time taken	1 hour
Grade	★	Postcode	RG26 5EB
Grid Ref	SU625571	Total climb	120 ft (37m)
Map	Ordnance Survey Explorer Map: 1:25000 scale – Sheet 144		
Terrain	A mix of concrete and woodland paths, which are mostly firm and dry. There are some uneven areas and the occasional tree root to negotiate. Some of the paths can get a little muddy after wet weather		
Obstacles	None		
Parking	From the Aldermaston Road, A340, between Sherborne St John and Tadley, 2.5 miles north of Basingstoke, turn east onto Morgaston Road. After 0.5 miles, turn right into a small parking area at Middle Gate (an entrance to Morgaston Woods). There's room for 4 or 5 cars here, however, if it's full there is scope to park along the road side. If you intend visiting The Vyne, then there is ample parking there; the walk can be accessed from the grounds adjacent to the lake at point 6		

This walk is a gentle amble around Morgaston Woods, which is part of the 1,120 acre Vyne estate. Morgaston is an enchanting wood comprising a diversity of trees. In spring, large areas of the wood are carpeted with native bluebells, together with a variety of other woodland wild flowers, including primroses, foxgloves, violets and common spotted orchids. Dead wood is mostly left in-situ to provide places for fungi to grow. You may also spot any of the three wild deer species (roe, muntjac and fallow) present in the woods.

The walk starts along a concrete track, constructed during the Second World War as a decoy to distract enemy bombers from local would be targets, and then continues past the formal grounds of The Vyne, with views over the grand lakeside house. From this point it's possible to access the grounds and to visit the house. The Vyne was built in the 16th century for Henry VIII's Lord Chamberlain, Lord Sandys. In 1653 the estate passed to Chaloner Chute who reduced and modernised the house and commissioned the classical portico on the north front. The Vyne was home to the Chute family for more than 350 years, then, in 1956, was given to the National Trust complete with furnishings and personal affects.

The route continues along 'Beech Ride' passing wetlands, which are visited by numerous wildfowl and wading birds, including coots, great crested grebes, heron, snipe, lapwing and redshank. There's a wooden hide just off the path, which is open for public use and has a lovely view out over the lake. As you continue, listen out for the distinctive plop of water vole jumping into the water at Wey Brook and look out for the remains of medieval fishponds, created in medieval times to supply the Lords table with fish, now less distinct as they were planted with poplars in the 1950s. The final leg of this route passes an open glade, which blooms with summer flowers attracting a diversity of butterflies.

Walk Description

S. From Middle Gate parking area, go through the wooden kissing gate and bear left to follow a concrete path into Morgaston Wood.

1. After 65 yards, at a junction, continue straight on as indicated by a brown arrow on a marker post to your left. Continue straight on past another turning to your right.

2. After 470 yards follow the concrete track round to the left past a corrugated iron wood shed. Keep left around the wood sheds, ignoring way marked turnings to your right. Continue along the concrete track, then after 300 yards follow the track as it turns to the right.

3. After another 80 yards, with a wooden gate 25 yards ahead, turn right onto a footpath, as indicated by a white arrow. After 120 yards, at a junction of paths, continue straight on to join a woodland track (with a drainage ditch on its left).

4. After 330 yards, at a junction, continue straight on, with black railings and parkland on your left, then a small display box containing a wasps nest on your right. This footpath was historically the main driveway to The Vyne and offers lovely views of the house.

5. After 165 yards, at the bottom of a gentle slope, in front of a lake, turn right onto Beech Ride, named after the beech trees planted both sides of the path.

6. Continue along Beech Ride with the lake on your left and, after 160 yards, you'll reach a wooden ramp on your left, leading down to a bird hide with an intimate view over the lake and wetlands. After taking in the scene from the hide, proceed along Beech Ride, then after 230 yards pass a small display box of feathers found on the estate. Continue straight on with Wey Brook, which feeds the lakes, on your left and passing two turnings to your right.

7. After almost 400 yards, where a pipe crosses under the path, you'll pass the medieval fishponds. To your right there's a gap in the bank which is an ancient dam that formed the ponds.

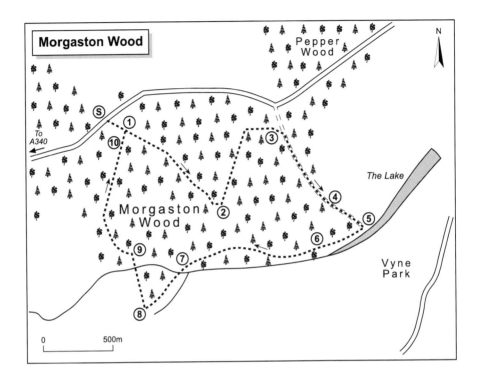

8. After another 210 yards follow the footpath round to the right, and up a gentle rise. After 210 yards, the path passes over a small culvert, which supplied water to the medieval fishponds.

9. Soon after, at a fork, turn left as indicated by a brown arrow on a marker post. Continue between two wooden posts to walk along an undulating path, then after 200 yards continue straight on at a crossing of paths, passing a small glade on you right, where numerous species of butterflies can be seen in the summer months.

10. After 315 yards, at a junction with the concrete track, turn left along the concrete track to return to Middle Gate at the starting point.

Refreshments

The Swan (1.8 miles)
3 Kiln Road, Sherbourne St John RG24 9HS
The Swan has a large, comfortable restaurant with attractive furnishings. The conservatory area is always popular and allows for more intimate dining. Children

are permitted in the main bar area which is very large and welcoming. There's also a large garden with plenty of picnic tables.
www.swan-pub-basingstoke.co.uk

Local Attractions

The Vyne
Sherborne St John, Basingstoke RG24 9HL
Originally built as a great Tudor 'power house', The Vyne was visited by King Henry VIII on at least three occasions and later became a family home, cherished by the Chute family for more than 350 years. The house is filled with an eclectic mix of fine furniture, portraits, textiles and sculptures. The attractive gardens and grounds feature an ornamental lake, delightful woodlands and flourishing wetlands, a haven for wildlife and water fowl.
www.nationaltrust.org.uk/main/w-thevyne

The grand 16th century house at The Vyne

28. Pamber Forest

Distance	2.7 miles (4.4km)	Time taken	1 hour 15 mins
Grade	★★	Postcode	RG26 3EQ
Grid Ref	SU617621	Total climb	95 ft (29m)
Map	Ordnance Survey Explorer Map: 1:25000 scale – Sheet 145		
Terrain	Sandy tracks, woodland paths. The path from the start point to the forest entrance has a 10% gradient for 200m, but all other paths on the trails are either flat or gently sloping. Although the paths are firm in dry weather, during wet weather, at any time of year, the site can be muddy		
Obstacles	None		
Parking	Pamber Heath is less than a mile from Tadley. Turn east off Aldermaston Road, A340, onto Silchester Road. Then after 1.2 miles, turn right onto Impstone Road. After 0.2 miles, just before the road bends to the right, park on the left at 'Pamber Forest and Silchester Common' gravel parking area		

Pamber Forest is a large ancient woodland, a remnant of the Royal Forest of Windsor, dating back to at least Norman times, when it was a royal hunting ground. Pamber is thought to take its name from the Old English Pennbeorg, meaning 'hill or barrow with an enclosure', and Baer meaning 'woodland swine pasture'.

The 478 acre site is now managed for conservation and visitors, using traditional coppicing and grazing, by Hampshire Wildlife Trust on behalf of Basingstoke and Dean Borough Council who lease it from the Englefield Estate. Oak and birch trees are predominant, some being over 300 years old. There are also areas of sweet chestnut and hazel. Pamber is enchanting whenever you visit; with carpets of wild daffodils in spring; purple heather and dancing butterflies through summer; colourful red and white fly agaric toadstools compliment the red and gold leaves in autumn months and in winter months beautiful frosted scenes make up for damp muddy days.

The route starts from Pamber Heath to walk down a bridleway alongside Lord's Wood to the entrance of Pamber Forest Reserve. This track can get muddy in winter months, making it very hard going with a pushchair, but is easily accessible during drier months. From here the route follows woodland footpaths to loop around the reserve, which is a haven for wildlife, including birds such as woodcock, siskins, a variety of warblers, nuthatch, tree creeper, three species of woodpecker, red kite, buzzards and tawny owls, and over 700 kinds of moths and butterflies, including silver-washed fritillary, purple hairstreak, white admiral, common fan-foot, and

String Lane Copse in Pamber Forest

the elusive purple emperor. The site was notified as a Site of Special Scientific Interest (SSSI) for its diverse flora and invertebrate populations.

There is a large network of wide surfaced tracks and smaller paths through the reserve, many of which are suitable for pushchairs for much of the year. The route takes in a diversity of woodland habitats, including woodland streams, dense ancient forest, a small pond, an open glade and patches of heathland grazed by Dexter cattle. Many dragonflies congregate about the ponds in late summer, including the red common, ruddy darters and, less frequently, the larger blue-grey hawker.

Walk Description

S. Take a public bridleway to the left of a 'Pamber Forest and Silchester Common' notice board. After 55 yards go through a small wooden gate and continue along the track.

1. After 450 yards, at the bottom of a hill, at a crossing of tracks (just before a large wooden bridge over a stream ahead), turn right to go through a wooden kissing gate into Pamber Forest Reserve. At this point you'll find a display board from which you can pick up a leaflet that includes a map of the forest.

2. Make your way along a footpath over a wooden platform to cross a stream. Then, after 80 yards, cross a path and bear right at a large looped fork in the

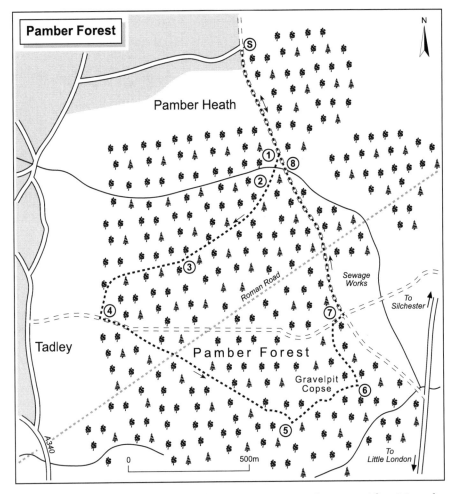

path, as marked with a blue bridleway arrow on a marker post. After 10 yards, continue past a red marker post. Then, after 375 yards, at a junction, continue straight on with a blue bridleway arrow on your right and a red marker post on your left.

3. Then, after 170 yards, at a crossing of paths, continue straight on, now with a wire fence on your left. After a further 325 yards follow the path round to the left, passing a marked footpath on your right.

4. After 200 yards, at a crossing of tracks, turn left, passing an information board on your right. Continue along the path, then after 140 yards bear right at a fork

in the path, as indicated by a red marker post. After another 500 yards, continue straight on at a crossing of tracks, again following the red marker posts. After 75 yards continue straight on, where a track crosses your way on a diagonal.

5. After another 340 yards, bear left at a fork in the path. Then after another 110 yards, go through the smaller of two wooden gates, and in 120 yards continue straight on at a crossing of paths.

6. After 130 yards turn left in front of a pond. Then after another 195 yards, continue straight on to walk along the right hand edge of a clearing.

7. Then, after 140 yards, at a junction with a gravel track, turn right in front of a wood shed. After 10 yards continue straight on past a turning to your left marked with a red post, and 25 yards further on pass another turning. Then turn left off the track to cross a corner of grass, and turn left to join a bridleway. Continue along the bridleway with a sewage works to your right, passing various turnings.

8. After 575 yards, continue across a wooden bridge over a stream, and proceed along the track, passing a kissing gate (where the route entered the reserve earlier) on your left. Continue up the hill, and after 485 yards go through the smaller of the two wooden gates and continue up the track to the parking area at the starting point.

Refreshments

The Calleva Arms
Silchester, Reading RG7 2PH
This pub overlooks the common and has an airy conservatory that overlooks its large enclosed garden. A good selection of food, including daily homemade specials and a 'for small fry' menu.
www.thecalleva.com

Local Attractions

Silchester Roman City Walls
Wall Lane, Silchester RG7 2HJ
Originally a tribal centre of the Iron Age Atrebates, Silchester became the large and important Roman town of Calleva Atrebatum. Unlike most Roman towns, it was never re-occupied or built over, so archaeological investigations give an unusually complete picture of its development. The amphitheatre was a place of entertainment and could accommodate between 3,500 and 7,250 spectators.
www.english-heritage.org.uk/daysout/properties/silchester-roman-city-walls-and-amphitheatre

29. Eversley, Warren Heath and Castle Bottom

Distance	5.2 miles (8.3km)	Time taken	3 hours
Grade	★★★★	Postcode	RG27 0PX
Grid Ref	SU779609	Total climb	140 ft (43m)
Map	Ordnance Survey Explorer Map 1:25000 scale - Sheet 159		
Terrain	Gravel paths and tracks, country roads and woodland footpaths. The section through Warren Heath is fairly flat but there are some hills around Castle Bottom National Nature Reserve		
Obstacles	There are two footbridges, just two railway sleepers wide on this walk; both are followed very closely by kissing gates making entrance into the gates a little awkward. The footbridges can be negotiated with a 3-wheel pushchair by lifting the rear wheels and pushing the pushchair across on its front wheel. Please take care to lock the front wheel and to keep the pushchair central on the footbridge. Take extra care in wet conditions as the surface may become very slippery		
Parking	Park at St Mary's Church parking area. Turn off the A327 just south of Eversley signed 'Eversley Barn Antiques' and 'Eversley Church'. Pass the antiques centre and a black barn then turn left opposite a black metal gate at the entrance to 'The Old Manor'		

Eversley is a small quintessential English village with its pond, cricket green, local stores and four pubs in the Blackwater Valley. St Mary's Church of Eversley has been a place of Christian worship for over 900 years and probably pagan before then. The current building dates mainly from the 18th century and has a long association with the village's most renowned resident, Charles Kingsley who was the rector in Eversley for some 31 years and was responsible for founding the village school in 1853. Charles Kingsley was also a notable author, naturalist and social reformer. His most famous book, *The Water Babies*, was written in 1862 for his youngest child, Grenville. In 1873 his powerful style of preaching was recognised in his appointment as a Canon of Westminster.

Starting at Eversley church this walk enjoys the gravel heathland tracks of Warren Heath, initially following 'Three Castles Path', a long distance route from Windsor to Winchester and then 'Welsh Drive' a historic route used by Welsh drovers when they brought their cattle to the markets in London. Although parts of the area are still being worked for gravel, the vast majority is being restored to create a diverse heathland forest, indeed these efforts have attracted a Sand and Gravel Association 'Restored Gravel Pit Award'.

After crossing Cooper's Hill Road, the route takes a scenic route around the outskirts of Castle Bottom National Nature Reserve, which supports a wide range of ecosystems, including one of the most important valley mires in southern England, with the associated heathland and woodland habitats. The reserve is of European importance for heathland birds and is a designated Special Protection Area (SPA). There is an option to enter the reserve but the various entrance points are not accessible for pushchairs, so little ones will need to disembark if you choose to explore the reserve itself.

On leaving the reserve the route crosses horse paddocks to follow a short section of country roads before joining a footpath through Up Green and around Lower Eversley Copse, which has a stunning carpet of bluebells in early summer, to return to Eversley church at the start point.

Walk description

S.   Leave the parking area heading towards St Mary's Church, and turn left onto the tarmac road, passing the church on your right. Follow this pretty country road for 525 yards to white metal gates at the entrance to 'Arletts Cottage'.

1.   Go through the gateway, then immediately turn left to follow a sandy footpath. After 165 yards, the path emerges from trees and becomes a little narrow and uneven for a short section but then opens out half way up the slope. At the top of the slope, at a fork, bear left, then almost immediately turn right to join a smoother path.

2.   Follow this path for 265 yards then, level with tall conifer trees to your right, bear left at a fork in the path. After a further 230 yards, at a major junction of tracks, there's a concrete pillar marking a 'Sand and Gravel Association Restored Gravelpit Award'.

3.   At this junction turn left onto a wide gravel track marked on a small post as 'Welsh Drive'. After 725 yards pass a 'Quarry Boundary Rules Apply' sign, and after another 25 yards continue straight on past a track to the right.

4.   Continue for a further 175 yards to pass the entrance to 'Bramshill Quarry' on your right, then proceed straight on past a small gate house and through white metal barriers.

5.   At a road, cross straight over (taking care as this is a fast road), to continue along 'Welsh Drive' on the other side of the road. Continue for 360 yards, through woodland to another road. Cross straight over passing four large

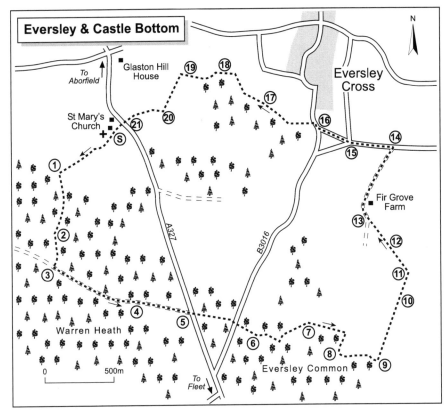

concrete blocks at the entrance to 'Bramshill Forest – Eversley Common Wood' (entrance sign to your right).

6. Continue straight on along a gravel track, then after 195 yards continue past a turning to your left, then immediately turn left onto another gravel track, marked footpath, heading diagonally away from the main track.

7. Continue past a quarry on your right and, after 455 yards, in front of wooden gates (an entrance to Castle Bottom National Nature reserve), turn right onto a gravel track. Continue along this track alongside the nature reserve and, after 300 yards, next to another entrance to the reserve, follow the track round to the right.

8. After 150 yards, follow the track around to the left and continue past a pretty wetland of reeds and young trees. Push up a short slope, then after 100 yards follow the track around to the right.

9. After another 75 yards, turn left onto a woodland track, and after 240 yards push up a steep hill. Then follow the track as it meanders through the woodland and, after 200 yards, you'll reach the final entrance to the reserve.

10. If you fancy venturing into the reserve your child will need to disembark whilst you lift the pushchair over the fence (it's lowest to the left of the gate). It's a short walk along a footpath to a wooden bench with great views over the heathland and trees, a great spot for a quick rest stop.

11. To continue along the route, walk past the gate (or if you've entered the reserve negotiate the gate onto the track and turn left). As the track bends to the right, bear left onto a gravel footpath. Then, after 125 yards, bear left at a fork and keep left as you continue down a slope.

A highland cow in the fields adjacent to Lower Eversley Copse

12. After 85 yards, bear slightly left to cross a narrow sleeper footbridge with great care (obstacle 1), and continue through the wooden kissing gate, marked with a yellow footpath badge. Then follow a grass footpath initially along the right hand edge of a field and, after 50 yards, bear slightly left to cross the field diagonally to a metal gate in the top corner of the field.

13. Go through a small wooden gate to the left of the metal gate. Then, bearing slightly left, follow a grass footpath across this second field, heading for the highest point in the field. Continue across the field to a small wooden gate to the left of a house and stables. Go through the kissing gate, then follow a narrow path for 5 yards to go down two small steps onto a tarmac drive.

14. Turn right onto the drive and continue past 'Kits Croft Lodge', then after 70 yards follow the road round to the right passing 'Firgrove Farm'.

15. After 535 yards, at a junction, cross directly over Firgrove Road to follow a footpath into trees, then immediately turn left onto a footpath running

adjacent to the road. After 50 yards, take care crossing a short railway sleeper footbridge, then after 35 yards pass a footpath on your right. After another 50 yards cross a roadside parking area with an entrance to 'Firgrove Manor' to your left. Continue along Firgrove Road (take great care as this is a reasonably fast road; walk on the left hand side to improve your visibility to oncoming traffic around the bend).

16. After 195 yards, continue straight across the top of a turning to Eversley and after 10 yards, at a cross roads, proceed straight over the road onto 'Up Green', which is a much quieter road.

17. After 250 yards, turn right onto Chequers Lane in front of 'High View' (an old timber frame house). Then, after 85 yards, turn left onto a tarmac drive, signed 'public footpath'. Continue past houses to go through a wooden kissing gate after 80 yards. Then follow a footpath along the edge of pasture fields, with 'Lower Eversley Copse' on your left.

18. After 370 yards, continue straight on to cross a gravel track. Then, after 330 yards, as you pass under electric cables, turn left onto a gravel track towards a metal gate. After just 15 yards, bear left to follow a footpath around the edge of the pasture fields, again with Lower Eversley Copse on your left.

19. After 75 yards, continue straight on past an electricity pylon to your left, then after a further 200 yards pass a footpath on your left (at the end of the woods). This next section gets muddy after rain and during winter months.

20. After another 135 yards, continue straight on past a footpath on your right to carefully cross a railway sleeper footbridge (obstacle 2), then immediately go through a wooden kissing gate. Take care as it's awkward turning into the kissing gate from the footbridge.

21. Continue straight on under electricity cables, alongside the left hand field boundary. After 35 yards turn left, again passing under the electricity cables, to walk along the left hand edge of another field, with a hedge on your left.

22. After 340 yards go through a wooden kissing gate, then immediately turn right to walk along the right hand field boundary (a wire fence and a line of oak trees). After 215 yards, go through another wooden kissing gate and continue straight on along a sand path with a line of trees on your right.

23. After another 140 yards go through a wooden kissing gate, then cross the A327 (with great care as this can be a busy road) to St Mary's Church green. Cross the green back to the parking area at the starting point.

Refreshments

The Frog and Wicket (1.8 miles)
The Green, Eversley Cross RG27 0NS
The Frog and Wicket is a genuine local traditional pub, situated opposite the oldest functioning cricket pitch in England. The bar areas serve a varied selection of seasonal light-bites, snacks and choices from the main and vegetarian menus. Fenced off and away from the main road, the beer garden has plenty of garden tables with umbrellas, a children's play area with climbing apparatus, a slide and a variety of other things to play with.
www.thefrogandwicket.co.uk

Local Attractions

Wellington Country Park (5 miles)
Odiham Road, Riseley, Nr Reading RG7 1SP
This is a 350-acre park with a wide range of activities and facilities including children's animal farm, miniature railway, adventure playground, nature trails, caféteria, picnic and BBQ area.
www.wellington-country-park.co.uk

Rycroft Equitation (1.8 miles)
New Mill Lane, Eversley, Hampshire RG27 0RA
Rycroft is a professional, family-run, British Horse Society approved, riding school. They cater for pleasure riders with excellent horses and are an ideal location for good hacking.
www.rycroft-equitation.co.uk

30. Yateley Common

Distance	2.2 miles (3.6km)	Time taken	1 hour 15 mins
Grade	★★	Postcode	GU17 0AW
Grid Ref	SU833592	Total climb	100 ft (30m)
Map	Ordnance Survey Explorer Map: 1:25000 scale – Sheet 145		
Terrain	Sandy tracks, gravel tracks, woodland paths. The walk is mainly level but also includes a number of minor hills		
Obstacles	None, other than the sand being a little tiring to push through in places. Care needs to be taken on a short section of raised board walks		
Parking	There are four parking areas at Yateley Common Country Park. This walk starts from a parking area off the A30, just less than a mile east of the junction between the A30 and the A327 (and Cricket Hill Lane). Steady your speed as the A30 becomes duel carriage, as the entrance to the parking area is just 0.2 miles further on, signed 'Yateley Common Country Park'. Turn up the track and, after 100 yards, in the first parking area, turn immediately left to go under a height barrier, then after 50 yards park in the second parking area		

Yateley Common offers 476 acres of heathland, woodland, grassland and ponds. Once infamous for highwaymen and smugglers, today the area attracts visitors for it's unspoilt heathland and natural history. This rare habitat is home to a diversity of wildlife including nightjars, garden warbler, chaffinch and stonechats. In spring you might hear the distinctive song of woodlark and Dartford warbler, and in summer months the contrast of purple heather and yellow gorse flower is spectacular, and the heathland is alive with butterflies such as silver studded blue and the grayling. The ponds on the common are picturesque and important for a number of scarce dragonflies and damselflies, including the black darter and downy emerald.

Much of the Common is designated as a Site of Special Scientific Interest and a Special Protection Area (SPA) because of its importance for wildlife. It has a dense network of bridleways with many smaller paths, many of which are suitable for pushchairs, although the sandy terrain can be tiring to push through.

This route starts with a gentle descent down a sandy gravel track, across beautiful heathland, to the pretty Stoud Pond, which is full of invertebrate life. The walk then follows a sandy bridleway, turning as it gets close to the A30 to climb through a wooded section before emerging onto open heathland. The heathland is managed to provide a variety of niches: bare ground providing nesting sites for woodlarks; young heather providing a breeding site for silver studded blue butterflies; and gorse scrub, ideal for the Dartford warbler.

The route continues along bridleways to Wyndham's Pool, which is a man-made pond constructed in the 1750s by Thomas Wyndham to supply fish ponds further down the valley. In the early 1900s the pond was used as a bathing pool; the remains of a diving board is still visible at the northern end. The pond supports a wealth of wildlife, including a variety of dragonflies, damselflies, wildfowl and grey heron, which can all be spotted from a lawned area next to the pond car park, which is a lovely place to stop for a picnic.

From Wyndham's Pool the route crosses an area known as Brandy Bottom where, in bygone times, smuggled brandy was stored on route to London. Emerging from trees the route continues across an area of open heathland, again dominated by heather, gorse, grass and small trees. The succession of the landscape to woodland is carefully managed to maintain the heathland which is so important for a diversity of highly adapted wildlife.

The route continues into a woodland known as the 'Old Ely', the site of the original Ely pub, the remains of which are still evident. The last section of the route is along raised and fairly narrow board walks, although wide enough for all-terrain pushchairs, care needs to be taken, especially in wet conditions when the wood may become slippery. At the time of going to press the board walks were under construction as part of a scheme to improve the footpaths in this area. The finished board walk will greatly improve ease of access along this section.

Walk Description

S. Follow a path just to the right of a 'Yateley Common Country Park' information board. After 65 yards, turn left onto a wider sandy path and, after another 45 yards, continue down a short hill. Halfway down, level with a conifer tree on your right, there's a lovely view over Strood Pool amongst trees at the bottom of the hill to your right. This pond is home to an abundance of pond life, including beautiful damsel and dragonflies.

1. At the bottom of the hill, with the pond on your right, turn left to join a wide sandy bridleway. Then, after 225 yards, as you get closer to the A30 above, merge with a path from the left. After another 75 yards, where the path forks into three, take the middle path to continue up a short slope. Then after a further 25 yards take either fork to go around a cluster of trees.

2. After 140 yards, bear right at a fork to follow a path along the line of telephone cables. After another 220 yards pass, under the telephone cables.

3. After a further 120 yards, at a fork in the path, in front of a muddle of telephone cables, bear right to merge with a gravel track from the right. After

just 10 yards, turn right onto another track, following a double set of telephone cables down a gentle slope.

After 160 yards, pass a bridleway on your left (with blue bridleway post to your right) and continue along the sand and gravel track through heathland of gorse, heather, shrubs and trees. After 265 yards, continue straight on to cross another bridleway.

4. After 120 yards, walk between short posts, with black railings on your right. Bear left as you reach a tarmac road to find a bridlepath to the right of a green 'Yateley Common Country Park' sign. Walk between more short posts, heading directly away from the cemetery. After 100 yards, continue straight on at a minor crossing of paths.

5. Then, after 85 yards, turn left onto a gravel path with Wyndham's Pool ahead on your left. After another 50 yards walk, over a concrete platform (noted to be the remains of a diving board).

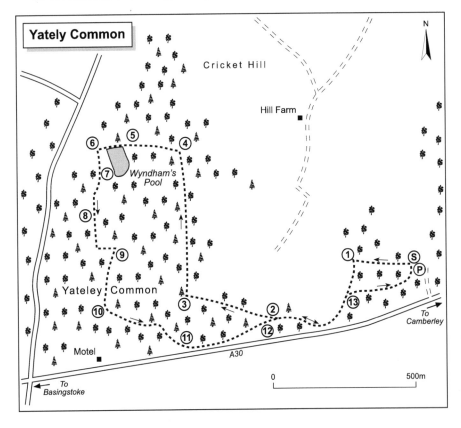

Wynhams Pool

6. After another 50 yards, continue straight on past steps on your left. Then, at the top of a short slope, turn left onto a gravel track into Wyndham's Pool parking area. Head straight across the parking area, towards a notice board.

7. Pass the notice board on your right to follow a narrow footpath across a grass lawn. This is a great spot for a picnic. Continue along the footpath into trees, then after 210 yards join a gravel track with a red brick house on your left.

8. After a further 35 yards, just before the track turns left, continue straight on to join a footpath, passing a round road viewing mirror on your right. Then, after 135 yards, at a crossing of paths, turn left onto a gravel track.

9. After 65 yards at another crossing, turn right off the bridleway. And, after 55 yards, pass a turning on your right, then continue forward under telephone cables.

10. After 150 yards, at a crossing of tracks, turn left as indicated by a blue bridle way arrow. Then, after another 110 yards, bear left at a fork, again as indicated by a blue bridleway arrow. After 50 yards, at a junction, turn right towards a woodland 50 yards ahead. Continue straight on into the woods, then after 25 yards bear right at a fork in the footpath.

11. After another 120 yards, at a junction, turn right to follow a bridlepath parallel to the A30 (some way to your right). Then pass a small red brick building on your left after 25 yards. After another 225 yards, continue straight on at a crossing of paths.

12. Then, after a further 140 yards, continue straight on to merge with another path and then walk under telephone cables. After 65 yards, take either fork to go around a small clump of trees, then after another 55 yards bear left at a fork and continue down a short slope.

13. After another 145 yards, bear right at a fork to walk along a raised board walk. Take care along this short section, and on similar board walks ahead, as they're fairly narrow. After 35 yards, at the end of the first board walk, continue along the path and up a short slope, then after 45 yards follow the path around to the left, and continue onto a second board walk. Another 250 yards takes you back to the parking area at the starting point.

Refreshments

The Ely (0.8 miles)
London Road, Blackwater, Camberley, GU17 9LJ
A traditional English country hotel and pub with beamed ceilings, red-brick walls covered in ivy, pan-tiled roof and a friendly atmosphere. The Ely offers a full range of bar and restaurant meals with a garden for summer dining.
www.elyhotel-yateley.co.uk/restaurant-and-bar-menus.php

Attractions

Trilakes Country Park (3 miles)
Yateley Road, Sandhurst GU47 8JQ
Trilakes Country Park incorporates an animal park, nationally renowned fishing lakes, café and an indoor children's soft play centre. The Water's Edge café provides snacks, drinks, meals and ice creams. The site itself is set in 19 acres of beautiful countryside including two stunning lakes.
www.blackwater-valley.org.uk/trilakes.htm

Horseshoe Lake Activity Centre (3.4 miles)
Mill Lane, Sandhurst GU47 8JW
Surrounded by open scenic countryside, the Centre operates on a 22-acre lake offering dinghy sailing, windsurfing, kayaking, canoeing, dragon boating and raft building. The team at Horseshoe Lake Activity Centre can provide private tuition, one off taster sessions, progressive weekly courses or multi-activity packages.
www.freetimewatersports.co.uk